THE ARCHAEOLOGY OF IRELAND

The Archaeology of Ireland

PETER HARBISON

Drawings by
SHIRLEY FELTS

CHARLES SCRIBNER'S SONS · New York

FRONTISPIECE
The megalithic tombs
called court-cairns,
like this one at Creevykeel,
Co. Sligo, are man's
earliest stone structures
to survive in Ireland.

1 3 5 7 9 11 13 15 17 19 I/C 20 18 16 14 12 10 8 6 4 2

Printed in Great Britain
Library of Congress Catalog Card Number 75-38405
ISBN 0-684-14593-6

CONTENTS

ACKNOWLEDGMENTS

Thanks are due to John McCarthy, Commissioner of Public Works, for permission to include discussion of unpublished material excavated by members of his staff; to Tom Fanning, Barry Raftery and David Sweetman for having checked that part of the text concerning their respective excavations and for their permission to include as yet unpublished data from them; to Brian Lynch, Leo Swan, Laurence Flanagan, Joseph Raftery, Breandán Ó Riordáin, John Hunt and Jim Bambury who went to considerable personal trouble to provide photographs for this volume.

Thanks are also due to the following for permission to reproduce black-and-white photographic material: Commissioners of Public Works in Ireland, frontispiece and pages 9, 31, 32, 34, 37, 56, 67, 68, 91, 93, 95, 99, 102; Bord Fáilte, pages 10 and 104; Royal Society of Antiquaries of Ireland, pages 14, 15, 16, 45; Shannon Free Airport Development Company, pages 21 and 74; Leo Swan and the Director, Ordnance Survey of Ireland, pages 22 and 23; Leo Swan and Seámus Caulfield, page 24; Professor M. J. O'Kelly, page 41; National Museum of Ireland, pages 46, 48, 58, 61, 70, 72; Noel Mitchell, page 50; Northern Ireland Department of Finance and Dudley Waterman, page 51; Leo Swan, pages 53 and 63; Ulster Museum, page 65; Royal Irish Academy, page 70; Breandán Ó Riordáin and the National Museum of Ireland, pages 78, 81, 83, 85, 89; Department of Aerial Photography, Cambridge, page 101; St Andrews Institute of Maritime Archaeology, pages 107 and 109; Marc J. Jasinski, pages 113 and 115.

Thanks for permission to use coloured photographic material are due to: Bord Fáilte, jacket photograph and facing pages 48, 65, 80; National Museum of Ireland, facing pages 49, 64, 96; Trinity College, Dublin, facing page 81; National Maritime Museum, Greenwich, facing page 97 (*top*); Ulster Museum facing page 97 (*bottom*).

The drawing on page 47 is based on one in H. Maryon's *Bronze Age Workshop*.

The publishers have made every effort to trace the owners of copyright material appearing in this book. In the event of any question arising as to the use of such material, the publishers, while expressing regret for any error unconsciously made, will be pleased to make the necessary correction in any future edition.

INTRODUCTION

For an island of its size, Ireland possesses a great wealth of arch-aeological material, ranging from objects recovered from the earth and now stored in museums, to old tombs, earthworks, castles and abbeys which provide us with an important visual backdrop for the stage on which Irish history was played. An academic interest in this material can be attested as far back as 1191 when the *Annals of Loch Cé* recorded the finding of an axe and a spearhead in the bed of the River Galway. Many centuries later, in 1545, we find a description in the *Annals of the Four Masters* of the contents of a bishop or archbishop's tomb in Christchurch Cathedral in Dublin.

But it was not until the eighteenth century that such isolated instances became more commonplace and that there arose a more widespread awakening of interest in the history and the origins of the physical remains of Ireland's past. Those who dabbled in the subject of antiquity two centuries ago were dilettanti and amateurs, whose speculative imagination was far stronger than their know-ledge. The nineteenth century brought with it a more factual approach. When George Petrie, a draftsman of Scottish origin, was working for the Historical Commission of Ireland's first Ordnance Survey between 1833 and 1839, he scoured the countryside for prehistoric and Early Christian antiquities, and the extensive notes and drawings which he and his colleagues made of them at the time have become invaluable records, not only because they form the first extensive survey of Irish monuments, but also because they describe some items which have long since vanished. Petrie's work on Tara, as well as on the Round Towers and early ecclesiastical architecture of Ireland, published in 1838 and 1845 respectively, has rightly earned for him the title of 'Father of Irish Archaeology'.

1849 saw the foundation of the Kilkenny Archaeological Society which later developed into the country's premier archaeological body, the Royal Society of Antiquaries of Ireland. This society's *Journal*, of which more than a hundred volumes have appeared, is the greatest source of archaeological information in the country. Together with the *Proceedings of the Royal Irish Academy*, and a host of local journals, of which those covering Ulster, Louth, Kildare, Cork, Kerry and North Munster can be singled out for special mention, it has given us the publication not only of excavations, but also of individual studies on artefacts, buildings and art history which form the backbone of our archaeological knowledge of Ireland today.

During the nineteenth century, the Royal Irish Academy did marvellous work in gathering together a very comprehensive collection of portable antiquities, many of which are now on display in the National Museum of Ireland in Dublin. The Catalogue of this collection was published in three volumes between 1857 and 1863 by Sir William Wilde, the father of Oscar Wilde. This was a work almost unequalled anywhere in Europe in its day, and although the expansion of the collection in the meantime has rendered it somewhat obsolete, it is nevertheless one of the most outstanding reference works of the nineteenth century on Irish archaeology.

Every science must have its birth pangs, and the science of excavation is no exception. The excavations which took place in Ireland in the last century were, as elsewhere, inadequate by modern standards, being in many cases little more than planned robberies. It was not until men like George Coffey, the Curator of Antiquities in the National Museum in Dublin, began excavating in the 1890s that a higher standard of excavation and its ensuing publication emerged. This trend was followed by R. A. S. Macalister who, in 1909, was created the first Professor of Archaeology in the recently established National University of Ireland, though the excavations which he carried out in the following thirty-five years were not always as meticulous as they might have been. Macalister wrote some interesting works of synthesis on Irish archaeology, but like many books of their kind, their conclusions were often weakened by subsequent research. His dominance of the Irish archaeological scene in the first thirty years of this century should not, however, be allowed to obscure the great and largely unsung survey work on Irish forts, megalithic tombs, castles and churches which was carried out by Thomas Johnson Westropp from 1890 till his death in 1922.

The 1930s saw the dawn of the first truly scientific excavations in Ireland, and a new standard in their publication. From 1932, E. Estyn Evans, a geographer who has earned for himself the reputation of doyen of Irish archaeology, began an important series of excavations with his colleague Oliver Davies which explored the country's earliest megalithic tombs, known as court-tombs or court-cairns. In 1932, the Harvard University Archaeological Mission came to Ireland and, under the leadership of Hallam J. Movius and Hugh Hencken, carried out what have since become some of Ireland's most 'classic' excavations on sites such as Poulawack and

Professor O'Kelly's excavations of the Neolithic mound at Newgrange uncovered the massive stones forming the roof of the passage to the burial chamber.

Ballinderry. Such great developments helped in moulding a new and well-trained school of Irish excavators. These included men like G. F. Mitchell who excavated Stone Age settlements, Seán P. Ó Ríordáin, who conducted excavations around Lough Gur in the 1940s and on Tara Hill in the 1950s, Joseph Raftery who worked largely on Iron Age sites, and M. J. O'Kelly, whose range of activities extended from the exploration of Stone Age tombs to late medieval fortifications.

From their important positions in universities and museums, these men passed on the experience they gained to their pupils, too numerous to mention individually, who continue to keep up the high standards set by their teachers. This has led to an extremely healthy body of young Irish excavators who are daily involved in the task of bringing more material to light which helps in elucidating the country's past. Every year between thirty and forty excavations are carried out in Ireland, and summary reports of these are produced each year in the Association of Young Irish Archaeologists' valuable publication entitled *Excavations*.

The archaeologists of the 1930s and 1940s chose their own sites because they wanted to clarify certain academic problems which interested them. In 1953 the Office of Public Works inaugurated at Mellifont a new type of excavation at National Monuments sites which continues to flourish, and which served the purpose of providing more accurate information for the subsequent conservation of buildings. But in the last decade, the choice of archaeological sites to be excavated has been increasingly determined by the desire to save valuable material in advance of its destruction by the tentacles of the mechanical digger. The inevitable modern development which led to these 'rescue digs' was not confined to agricultural improvement in the countryside, but is now becoming more acute in Ireland's medieval towns. The National Museum of Ireland's rescue excavation of parts of the old city of Dublin around Christchurch Cathedral, in advance of road-building and the erection of new civic offices, started in 1962 and is still continuing. It has already yielded very beneficial results and a wealth of finds, as well as making the public more aware of the value of what can be destroyed in digging the foundations of modern buildings. Ireland's first taste of urban archaeology in Dublin has recently led to excavations in other medieval Irish towns such as Carrickfergus and Cork.

But the increase in digging activity necessitated by these rescue operations brings with it more material which ought to be published, and the pressure to be in ahead of modern development compels excavators to spend much of their time rescuing one site after another at the expense of publishing those which they have already dug. This vicious circle has the unfortunate consequence that more and more excavated sites remain unpublished (except in summary form), to the great detriment and loss of Irish archaeology.

It is impossible to condense the published results of all this excavation activity of the last half-century into a volume of this size. Instead, a representative selection has been chosen, covering the period from the Stone Age up to the Spanish Armada of 1588, and through these an attempt is made to bring out some of the characteristics of each individual era which that time-span encompasses. It is hoped that the book will thus provide a useful introduction to the archaeology of this fascinating country, without resorting to a purely hand-book approach which can sometimes be a trifle dull and unexciting.

The ruins of Mellifont Abbey today, with the octagonal lavabo at the far end of the cloister garth, as seen from the north transept of the church.

1

When Did Man First Arrive in Ireland?

Ireland was not always as it is today, a country of comparatively few trees and with a patchwork quilt of fields partitioned by thick hedges and stone walls. As late as the sixteenth century, it had much more extensive forests which were cut down for boat-building and mining purposes—and also to deny shelter to rebels and outlaws who used them as a refuge. But in comparison to the length of time in which man has inhabited this planet, even those forests were comparatively young. Some 20,000 years ago—during the Palaeolithic or Old Stone Age—much of the country, except for the southern rim, was covered by massive glaciers which can scarcely have provided the wherewithal for man to live. However, at the same period man was already producing his first great works of art by painting animals in the caves of the warmer landscapes of France and Spain. Because Ireland was comparatively remote and difficult of access over the ice-cap which covered it, man may not have reached it by that time, and indeed it would appear to have been one of the last countries in Europe to have been colonised by man.

In 1928, John Kaye Charlesworth—a geologist—suggested that if there were any traces of man in Ireland dating from the Palaeolithic or the Ice Age, then there was at least a sporting chance that they would be found in the belt running along the south coast which had been left free of ice during the last glaciation. Charlesworth's suggestion was enough to lure members of the Bristol Speleological Society to the south of Ireland in the summer of that year to put his theory to the test. This society was devoted to the exploration of caves, and under the direction of E. K. Tratman, then as now an enthusiastic potholer, it set out to scour Co. Waterford for a suitable cave to excavate.

The principal archaeological sites of Ireland discussed in this book.

13

Movius's 1934 re-excavation of Kilgreany Cave in progress.

After visiting a number of caves in the county, Tratman settled upon one at a place called Kilgreany near the village of Cappagh. His instinct did not fail him, for he came upon numerous indications of human habitation in the course of his excavations in the cave. Hearths in which prehistoric men had lit their fires survived in three separate layers, of which the topmost one, belonging to the Bronze or Iron Age, was very much disturbed. The one below it was disturbed too, and it proved to belong to the Neolithic or Late Stone Age, as was demonstrated by a typically Neolithic polished stone axe which came to light in the same level as the hearth. Resting on this second hearth was the skull and some of the bones

14

of a woman—known as Skeleton A—which had also been disturbed, apparently by animals. The excavator noticed that there were cuts on the skull and some of the limb bones, and seeing also traces of burning on some of the skull fragments, he surmised that the woman may have fallen a victim to cannibalistic practices, while admitting at the same time that the cuts and the burning might just as well have been accidental. Below this second hearth was a stalagmite layer, formed by a constant drip from the roof. This layer Tratman considered to have been unbroken over the entire surface of the cave, so that he presumed that what was underneath this layer was intact and undisturbed. A third hearth was found under a part of the stalagmite layer which was made of a substance called tufa, for the formation of which a drip from the roof was also responsible. In the same stratum as the hearth were the remains of animals which would normally live only in icy conditions, including reindeer, brown bear, arctic lemming and the famous Irish elk with its enormous and awe-inspiring antlers. More important than this was the discovery of another human skeleton—Skeleton B—in the top

When the Harvard expedition reached the back of Kilgreany Cave, debris on the cave floor was almost two metres deep.

The bones of a giant deer were exposed in the 1934 excavation when the lower stalagmite was carefully chipped away near the entrance to the cave.

part of the lower stalagmite layer, and this skeleton must have been buried at much the same time that the third and lowermost hearth was in use. The fact that Skeleton B was in a layer which contained the bones of late Pleistocene—or Ice Age—animals led Tratman to conclude with delight that he had found for the first time proof of the presence of man in Ireland in late Pleistocene times—in other words, at the time when glaciers covered most of the country, except for the area near the south coast.

But Tratman's view did not go unchallenged. One man who was not convinced was the American archaeologist Hallam J. Movius. He was one of the leaders of the Harvard Archaeological Mission to Ireland which conducted a number of important excavations in the country from 1932 to 1938 and which, by employing a number of up-and-coming young Irish archaeologists, contributed very substantially to the development of a native school of trained excavators well versed in the latest techniques, some of whom we shall encounter later in this book. Tratman had only been able to excavate a part of the cave at Kilgreany during his season in 1928, and now, seven years later, Movius, who was on the threshold of gaining an international reputation as an expert on the Old Stone Age, set about excavating the remainder. In the course of his diggings, Movius concluded that Tratman's stalagmite layer did not cover the whole extent of the cave, and that it was in fact as much disturbed as the layers above it. It proved to contain an amber bead and Neolithic pottery which could not possibly belong to the Old Stone Age. He found that the bones of the arctic fauna were intermingled with those of domestic ox, and as domesticated oxen were not introduced until the Late Stone Age, he maintained that Skeleton B, which had been found in the same layer as the bones of the arctic animals, could not be claimed to belong to the Early Stone Age. Furthermore, Movius found that the charcoal of the hearth of this layer was of ash and oakwood, which could not have grown in the tundra conditions of the Ice Age and must therefore be later than the Ice Age. He also pointed out that no implements of the Early Stone Age had been found in the excavations, and that the skulls of skeletons A and B were of the same type, thus supporting their closeness in time. Expressing himself cautiously in a book which he wrote about the Irish Stone Age in 1942, Movius stated that he was more than reluctant to admit that man was in Ireland at the same time as the arctic lemming. In short, he doubted that Skeleton B belonged to the Old Stone Age, and implied that it must belong to the Neolithic period. It should be pointed out, however, that Tratman and Movius excavated in different parts of the cave, and that it is not easy to correlate the two parts.

These explorations by Tratman and Movius were carried out before the discovery of modern scientific dating techniques such as measuring the content of Carbon 14 in organic material, or measuring the amount of fluorine that has accumulated in bones; such techniques are still not perfected by any means, but they help to provide an absolute dating that is independent of the archaeological findings. More than twenty years after their discovery, the two skeletons from Kilgreany were submitted for dating by one or other of these two techniques. Different parts of Skeleton A, which by general consensus was assigned to the Late Stone Age Neolithic level, were dated by Kenneth Oakley in the British Museum's radiocarbon laboratory to 2630 ± 150 BC, a date perfectly in accordance with what could have been expected for Neolithic man. Unfortunately, the crucial Skeleton B could not be radiocarbon-dated because the radiocarbon content of the skull would automatically have been distorted by the waxy preservative coating

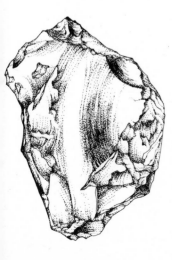

Palaeolithic flint from Mell near Drogheda: one of the oldest man-made implements known from Ireland.

'Bann flakes' of flint were among the most characteristic implements of the Middle Stone Age in Ireland.

which had had to be applied to it when it was originally discovered. Instead, following fluorine and nitrogen replacement tests on the bones, Dr Oakley suggested that the skeletal material might be older than 9000 BC and thus right back in the Old Stone Age where Tratman had placed it originally. So we still cannot say with any certainty whether Skeleton B from Kilgreany is the remains of Ireland's oldest known man, dating from the Ice Age. But despite that, it is still possible that it was he who killed the arctic animals whose bones were found in the cave. For the moment, therefore, archaeology cannot satisfactorily answer the question as to whether man lived in Ireland during the Ice Age.

More recently, Professor G. F. Mitchell, the leading authority on the Older Stone Age in Ireland, was out collecting stones from a quarry at Mell, less than a mile north-west of Drogheda, when he found a flint flake which was undoubtedly struck by human hands, and which seemed to belong to the Palaeolithic or Old Stone Age. However, the gravel among which it was found probably originated not at Mell but from dry land which has since sunk below the Irish Sea. The implement could have been picked up by the glaciers when they were advancing down the bed of the Irish Sea, possibly before 25,000 BC, and deposited with the gravel at Mell when the ice of the glacier melted on its retreat northwards. This flake implement, whatever its original purpose may have been, shows us at least that during the Old Stone Age man had penetrated as far westwards as what is now the basin of the Irish Sea. It cannot be taken as irrefutable evidence that Palaeolithic man actually got to Ireland; but taken together with Tratman's excavations and Oakley's fluorine replacement test on Skeleton B from Kilgreany, it makes the suggestion less unlikely. It certainly does not exclude the possibility that some day we may yet find more definite evidence to show whether man came to Ireland during the Ice Age.

Apart from these somewhat contentious remains, the earliest reliable traces of human activity which we have in Ireland date from around 6800 BC. At that time the sea was possibly as much as twenty-five metres lower than it is now, and the stretch of water between Northern Ireland and Scotland was consequently considerably narrower than it is today. This would have meant an easier and less hazardous passage for those who were brave enough to row across the troubled waters of the North Channel. This was almost certainly the route which was being used by small families who were arriving in Ireland from south-western Scotland at around this time, and it is

In the fourth millennium BC the older Mesolithic hunting population adopted new implements such as the core-axe and the fish-tail scraper.

more than mere coincidence that the very few sites known to belong to this period are largely clustered around the head of the Irish Sea near where they landed. There was, however, another good reason why they should have concentrated their hunting activity in this region. Antrim, Ireland's most north-easterly county, is rich in flint, and this was the best-known material used by man in the Mesolithic or Middle Stone Age in Ireland from about 6800 BC until the fourth millennium BC. Often the only visible remnants of man's activity on Mesolithic sites are the numerous implements made from flint or chert. One of the most common of these was a flake, known as a Bann flake after the river valley in which it most frequently occurs. It was a leaf-shaped blade, fashioned by broad strikes and then re-worked near the striking platform. These flakes may have been used as knives, but could also have served as the heads or prongs of fishing spears.

After the initial influx of people using such flint implements around 6800 BC, there appear to have been comparatively few new immigrants for a further three thousand years. Those who had come originally must have been small in number by modern standards, but nevertheless sufficiently numerous to ensure the line of succession for a further three thousand years. Theirs was a hard life—moving from place to place without having any permanent home, catching and smoking fish, and having to be constantly on the look-out for roving animals whose meat could help them to survive. Their traces become much more common in the period after 3500 BC, when we find them occupying not only their original heartland in counties Antrim, Down and Derry, but moving south along the coast as far as Dalkey Island at the mouth of Dublin Bay, and venturing as far inland as the Inny lakes not far from Mullingar and as far west as Lough Gara on the Sligo/Roscommon border. In the period after 3500 BC, these Mesolithic hunters and fishers adopted new types of tools such as large core-axes, boring tools and scrapers in the form of a fish tail. What led them to adopt these new implements is difficult to say, but we might surmise that the reason why they drifted from their original bridgeheads in north-eastern Ireland further south down the coast and into the Irish midlands was that they were displaced by newly arrived groups who had begun to occupy parts of Ulster by about 3700 BC, when the Neolithic or New Stone Age dawned in Ireland.

2

The First Farmers and the Giants of the Boyne Valley

By 3700 BC new settlers had begun to arrive in Ireland who were destined to bring about great changes in the way of life and the landscape of the country. We cannot say to what race they belonged or what language they spoke. In contrast to the Mesolithic hunting and fishing folk whom we encountered in the last chapter, they were farmers—Ireland's first. Whereas the Mesolithic population had core-axes made from flint, these newcomers were characterised by their use of polished axes, made of a variety of stones including porcellanite which they were to mine at Tievebulliagh in Co. Antrim. This adoption of polished stone implements marks the change from the Mesolithic to the Neolithic. However, the Neolithic population also mined flint and made new forms with it, of which the flint arrowhead is the most notable. Instead of having to rely solely on wild animals for their meat diet, the Neolithic communities had domesticated animals such as oxen and sheep. While they probably moved their herds from one place to another to some extent, they were not continually on the move as the earlier Mesolithic people had been. After the arrival of these new farmers, the old Mesolithic population must have continued to carry on their specialised form of fishing before they were finally absorbed into the Neolithic stock. With their polished axes, the newly arrived agriculturalists gradually—if not actually immediately—set about clearing some of the trees which had grown up and spread after the retreat of the glaciers. In these cleared glades they planted crops such as barley and later also wheat. Their crops and herds of domesticated animals allowed them to settle in one place for a

A modern reconstruction of a Neolithic round house erected near the shores of Lough Gur around 1946 shows a network of roof-timbers which were covered by thatch.

considerable time. It was the start of settled community life in Ireland.

In 1967–68 Arthur ApSimon, formerly of Queen's University in Belfast and now a lecturer at the University of Southampton, brought to light in his excavations at Ballynagilly near Cookstown in Co. Tyrone the earliest settlement of these Neolithic men known in Ireland. At first they do not appear to have built any stable form of habitation, but may have housed themselves in some form of covered pits. Charcoal from one of these pits gave a radiocarbon date of 3675 ± 50 BC which, if it is correct, is the earliest radiocarbon date of any Neolithic occupation site anywhere in Ireland or Britain. It was not for some centuries, apparently, that the inhabitants built a wooden house on the site. This house was almost square in plan, measuring 6·5 by 6 metres. The two longer walls were embedded in a trench about 30–40 cms wide and 20–30 cms deep. Into this trench, planks of radially-split oakwood had been placed vertically, and stones were packed round the planks to bed them in properly. The charcoal from the planks gave a radiocarbon date of 3215 ± 50 BC. There was one post-hole near the west end of the southern trench, and other possible post-holes were found inside the house, in which the roof-supports must once have rested. The

Ranging rods help to emphasise the room divisions in the ground-plan of this Late Stone Age house at Bally-glass. The small stones were used as footings for the wall-timbers of the house.

discovery of a Neolithic house made of planks came as a considerable surprise, as no Neolithic site in Britain or Ireland had produced a house of this nature. Some sherds of Neolithic pottery were found in the trenches of the house and in a pit inside the house, demonstrating that pottery was already being made at that period in Ireland. There were at least two hearths within the house, and three leaf-shaped arrowheads also came to light. The existence of such early traces of Neolithic settlement in Northern Ireland suggests that the Neolithic farmers may have used the same access route across the North Channel as did their Mesolithic antecedents. It was possibly from the Yorkshire Wolds—where similar pottery is known—that they had emigrated before they embarked westwards across the Irish Sea.

Timbered houses also of Neolithic date, but probably later than that at Ballynagilly, had already come to light in the extensive excavations at Lough Gur in Co. Limerick which were carried out in the 1940s by the late Professor Seán P. Ó Ríordáin of University College, Dublin. Some of the houses at Lough Gur were rectangular, and others were round in plan. The photograph on page 21 shows the tentative reconstruction of one of these round houses;

it was built on the site according to the original measurements by Professor Ó Ríordáin and John Hunt. Unfortunately, this reconstruction, which was made for a film documentary, no longer exists.

Another house bearing a certain resemblance to that at Ballynagilly was found during excavations at Ballyglass near Ballycastle in Co. Mayo. There, in the years 1968 and 1970–71, Seán Ó Nualláin, working on behalf of the Ordnance Survey, discovered the remains of a timber house which, except at its northern end, was demarcated by a trench of much the same character as that of the Ballynagilly house. But at Ballyglass the house was markedly rectangular in shape, measuring 13 by 6 metres. Instead of being built of planks, it was made of poles which were placed at varying distances apart in the trenches, though we do not know what material was used to

Aerial photograph of the excavation at Ballyglass. The post-holes of the timber house (*centre foreground*) lie at an angle to the stone tomb with its oval central court.

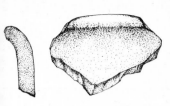

This pottery sherd found in the Ballyglass excavation has an out-turned rim typical of Neolithic pottery.

fill the spaces between the poles. The house had two smaller sub-divisions near its northern end, while at the southern end there was a small compartment which may have been accessible only from outside—perhaps a shed for cattle. The Ballyglass house, too, yielded its share of pottery, most of the sherds having out-turned rims in the typically Neolithic fashion. The house came to light almost accidentally, because it lay just beside a large megalithic tomb which was the prime object of the excavator's attention. Ó Nualláin found that the post-holes of the house had been later filled in. Having dug both house and tomb, he found it hard to escape the conclusion that the house was intentionally demolished to make way for the construction of the tomb, as this seemed the best explanation as to why the post-holes of the house had been filled in. The question can at least be asked if this was a house in the conventional sense of a permanent human habitation, or whether it may not have served as a kind of primitive temple, whose site was regarded as so sacred that an important burial place (and possibly also ritual site) was later built of more durable stone in the same precinct?

The same area in Co. Mayo is also proving to be rich in prehistoric remains of a different kind. Today, a considerable amount of the land in the vicinity is covered by peat bog which began to form around the second millennium BC, possibly due to a change in weather conditions. This serves as a wonderful sealing layer for anything which existed on the ground before the peat began to accumulate three thousand or more years ago. The task of un-covering some of what lies beneath the peat has been undertaken over the past few years by Dr Michael Herity and Seámus Caulfield, both lecturers in archaeology in University College, Dublin.

At Belderg Beg, Seámus Caulfield discovered Stone Age plough marks, cultivation ridges and traces of a circular house bounded by stone walls, shown in the north western section of the photograph.

At his native heath of Belderg Beg, Mr Caulfield found a number of tillage plots partitioned off by stone walls, and beside these there was a Bronze Age circular structure of stone and earth, nine metres in diameter and with a paved entrance. A wall trench inside the circle was filled with charcoal, showing that this was the remains of a house or possibly a granary built of timber; inside were some querns and the stone rubbers used to grind grain on them. But even more significant than the timber structures were the unequivocal traces of early agricultural activity on the site in the form of plough marks criss-crossing one another in the ground. These are the earliest plough marks known anywhere in Ireland. Above them were ridges and furrows, showing a system of crop-growing unexpectedly advanced at such an early period. The crops were planted on the ridges, and the furrows were a useful way of draining away any surplus water. Dr Herity uncovered further ridges and furrows not very far away at a place called Carrownaglogh. At Behy, also in Co. Mayo, a field wall made of stone had abutted on to a megalithic tomb of the same general type as that at Ballyglass, and it seemed as if stones from the tomb had been robbed to build the field walls, suggesting that at least in this instance, the field walls were a later development than the great stone tombs of the Neolithic Age.

Megalithic tombs are places of burial built of massive stones, and about 1,200 examples of various types are known in Ireland. Among the earliest are the so-called court-cairns—mounds of stone heaped over long rectangular stone-built burial chambers fronted by a semi-circular open space or court flanked by standing stones. In some cases, as at Ballyglass, two court-cairns would be placed face to face; so that the tomb would consist of a large open oval court in the centre with burial chambers at either end. These tombs were communal burial places. Sometimes the bones or cremated remains of one generation of dead were brushed aside to make room for the deposition of later burials, so that these great tombs must have been in use as cemeteries for many decades if not indeed centuries. Many hundreds of tons of stone had to be moved and levered into position in the course of the construction of these tombs, and the society which built them must have been very well organised and have had considerable manpower at its disposal to have carried out such large-scale architectural projects.

The greatest monuments to the building genius of Neolithic man in Ireland are to be found in yet another type of megalithic tomb called passage graves, which were built by a different race from that of the court-cairn builders. Like the court-cairns, these passage graves were also communal burial places. They are sited normally on hill-tops, and consist of large round earthen mounds with a long passage leading from the edge of the mound to a tomb at or near the centre of the mound. About three hundred such passage graves are known in Ireland, most of them in the northern half of the country, often clustered together in what are loosely termed cemeteries. The most imposing of these cemeteries is the one sited on three neighbouring hills called Dowth, Knowth and Newgrange in a bend of the River Boyne between Drogheda and Slane in Co. Meath. The excavations which have been in progress since

1962 at the two latter sites, Knowth and Newgrange, have given us a tremendous insight into the origins as well as the architectural and artistic abilities of their builders.

Knowth is the westernmost of the three great passage graves on the Boyne. When R. A. S. Macalister, the first Professor of Archaeology in Dublin, did some trial digging there in the 1940s, he uncovered a number of decorated horizontal stones which had formed a retaining kerb round the base of the great mound. In 1962, Dr George Eogan of University College, Dublin, began the first of many seasons of exploration on the site. He faced a formidable task, as the site of the tomb and the area surrounding it which he wanted to uncover is six and a half acres in extent. The enormous burial mound itself covers an acre and a half. It has a maximum diameter of just over ninety metres, and is just over ten metres high. Before attacking the main mound, Dr Eogan started digging the area immediately surrounding it. He soon began to uncover a series of 'satellite' tombs (smaller passage graves) nestling outside the main mound like a lot of chickens round the mother hen. Where these 'satellite' tombs had not been damaged beyond recognition, they consisted, like the mother tomb, of a mound surrounded by a circular setting of kerb-stones. Each had a passage leading into a burial chamber which was either about the same width as the passage, or else was larger and rounded in shape, with smaller burial niches leading off from it. So far, sixteen of these 'satellite' tombs have been excavated.

The next stage in the excavation was to dig some trial trenches in the main mound itself, and to try to uncover all the kerb-stones which had surrounded the base. It turned out that the mound had been very carefully constructed, with successive layers of sods, stones, boulder clay and shale laid one on top of the other, looking in section like a multi-tiered chocolate cake. Each layer gradually thinned out and sloped downwards as it approached the edge of the mound.

When he started on the kerb, Dr Eogan discovered further kerb-stones which Macalister's trowel had missed: they were covered with a dazzling display of decorative motifs. These motifs, pocked out on the stone, are almost entirely geometrical in character, although some people, by a great effort of the imagination, claim to see a stylised representation of the human face on one of them. Circles and U-shaped motifs (sometimes concentric), spirals, snake-like zigzags, herring-bones, triangles and diamond-shapes ('lozenges') predominate, and some of these motifs were also found on stones in the 'satellite' tombs. The line of the kerb did not form a complete circle, but curved inwards in a few places. One of these places was at the northernmost extremity of the mound, where it swerved inwards to avoid what can only be presumed to have been a pre-existing 'satellite' tomb; this suggests that one at least of the 'satellites' had been built before the main mound. Only complete excavation of the mound down to the old ground surface can show whether there was anything else on the site of the mound before it was erected.

On the western side of the mound the kerb also curved inwards, and the kerb-stones grew in size as they approached the centre of the curve. A ditch has been dug inside the kerb here at a much later date, and occupational debris showed that the area had been inhabited in the Early Christian period. But further in, and leading towards the centre of the mound, there appeared a low passage constructed of dry-wall masonry of small stones. This passage was similar to that used in souterrains, or underground passages, which were known from elsewhere to be of the same Early Christian date as the occupational debris just inside the kerb; later, Dr Eogan was to find a number of these souterrains burrowed under the surface of the great mound itself like a rabbit warren. Unexpectedly, however, on July 11, 1967, Dr Eogan discovered that this poorly-built passage led to another one built of tall upright stones and covered by massive lintels. Penetrating further, he realised that he had accidentally come across the burial chamber itself: the passage led on in a straight line for about 26 metres and then turned slightly to the right, before gradually expanding into the burial chamber proper. The whole length of the passage and chamber together was about 34 metres.

Dr Eogan had discovered what was the longest passage grave then known. Just before the bend in the passage there was a large stone basin lying on the floor, and this had probably been dragged out from its original position in the chamber by some predator before being abandoned in the passage. The burial chamber proper was demarcated by a sill-stone lying on the ground just across the entrance to it. A number of stones in the passage and in the burial chamber were decorated with a variety of motifs, some of them hitherto unknown in the pattern book of passage-grave art. The most remarkable of these was in the right-hand wall just beyond the bend of the passage; it was a stylised form of the human face on

Symbolic geometrical designs carved on the stones of passage graves.

which two eyes were clearly visible on top. Looking like a wise old owl, but possibly intended as a symbolic representation of a god, it seems to have indicated to the intruder that he was now entering the chamber of the dead. The stone forming the back wall of the burial chamber was decorated with concentric rectangles. This motif also occurred on the kerb-stone immediately outside the entrance to the passage, which also had a groove running vertically down the middle of the stone—apparently an indication that behind this groove lay the centre of the entrance to the tomb.

The burial chamber and the passage with its characteristic bend had interesting parallels in Brittany, and hinted that the passage-grave builders may have come from there before finding their new home on the banks of the Boyne. Decoration of the same general nature can be found on a number of tombs around the Gulf of Morbihan on the southern coast of Brittany, and if the French radiocarbon dates for Breton passage graves are correct, it was there that passage graves were first built some time around 3800 BC. What it was that brought these men to Ireland we cannot say, nor can we say exactly how long after the building of the first passage graves they set out for Ireland; but they must have had strong reasons for doing so. Other passage graves in Spain and Portugal seem to have been built by men who already knew the use of metal, so one might suppose that the passage-grave migrants had come to Ireland in search of copper and gold; but no Breton or Irish passage graves have yielded any metal objects in a primary position in the tombs, so this supposition remains unlikely. We must presume that the men who mounted this massive operation of building these great tombs were men of the Stone Age, who used pointed stones to pock out the striking geometrical motifs that ornament the tombs. These decorations must have been of great religious significance. It is a pity that we do not have at our disposal a kind of pictorial Rosetta Stone with parallel images which could give us the key to the meaning of those mysterious symbols. Many and various attempts at interpretation have been made, but they are of necessity highly speculative, and the markings are still an enigma. They could however, be symbolic representations of the deities worshipped on the site, and of the world and the life that they created.

The floor of the passage and the chamber which Dr Eogan had discovered were covered in silt, in which the remains of burnt bone could be seen, suggesting that the builders had cremated their dead. But though Dr Eogan must have been tempted to drop everything

OPPOSITE
One of the three burial
niches opening off the
main chamber of the
tomb discovered at
Knowth in 1968.

else and start clearing out the passage and chamber straight away, he decided with exemplary restraint to complete his excavation of the circle of kerb-stones and to keep the best wine until last. Or so it seemed.

By the end of July the following year (1968), he had reached the opposite segment of the kerb-stone circle when he came upon yet another of those ubiquitous souterrains. This one ran inside and roughly parallel to the kerb of the mound. While excavating just to the south of this souterrain, Dr Eogan found a small hole appearing; it looked as if a lintel in the passage of the souterrain had collapsed there. On the following day, August 1 1968, it became possible to enter the passage at that point. And now came a truly dramatic development. The lintel proved to have belonged not to just one souterrain but to a spot where four separate passages converged. Three of these were of the same dry-stone construction as the other souterrains; but the fourth passage was totally different. It was constructed in the megalithic fashion of large upright stones. Following it inwards towards the centre of the mound, Dr Eogan discovered to his amazement that it was the passage of a second and totally unexpected tomb—unexpected because no other passage grave in Ireland or Britain was then thought to have concealed a second tomb within its mound. To add to the importance of the discovery, the plan of the second tomb differed completely from the one which he had found the previous year. It shared with the 1967 tomb the long passage of upright stones covered with lintels (the length of passage and chamber, in fact, was marginally greater than the 1967 tomb), and the two tombs must have been built almost back to back, with only a few metres between them. But the real difference between the two tombs lay in the burial chambers. Whereas the western tomb discovered in 1967 had a chamber that was little more than a broadening of the passage, the eastern chamber found in 1968 was roughly round in plan, and had three burial niches opening off it, one on each side at right-angles to the passage and the third at the back of the tomb. The passage gained in height as it approached the chamber, unlike the 1967 tomb, and crawling along it on all fours in the mud, as Dr Eogan recalled afterwards, 'I saw a massive chamber. I looked up at the corbelled vaulting and still could not believe how huge it was.' The roof was almost seven metres high, and had been constructed in the classic corbelling style—by stones being placed in a rough circle horizontally one above the other, with each layer projecting inwards above

The finely decorated ritual basin lying as it was found in the right-hand recess of the burial chamber discovered at Knowth in 1968.

the one below it until the stones met at the top in the centre. In the burial niche to the right there was a large stone basin which, though broken, still retained its beautifully balanced decoration of straight and curved lines. We can only surmise that such basins played an important ritual part in the burial ceremony. Many of the stones forming the walls and roof of both passage and chamber were decorated, and some of the stones were even inscribed with the names of the Early Christian Irish who had penetrated the tomb from the souterrains only about a thousand years ago.

The discovery of this second tomb under the mound came as a complete surprise, not only to Dr Eogan but to the whole archaeological world. It showed that both types of tombs represented among the 'satellites' were also represented in the main mound. The stone basin in the right-hand burial niche can certainly be reckoned as the most beautiful of its kind to have survived. While we will have to await the complete excavation of the mound to find out if

32

one of the tombs is earlier than the other, the likelihood is that they were contemporary. Since the cruciform plan of the 1968 tomb is of a type also known in Brittany, this may help to show that the Breton tombs with one or other of the ground-plan types represented at Knowth were also contemporary with each other in Brittany.

A further consideration after the discovery was that there might be other Irish passage-grave mounds with undetected double tombs. One of the likely candidates for this possibility was Newgrange, where the known passage and chamber only penetrated just a little less than half-way into the mound. Newgrange, which lies about a mile east of Knowth, is the second of the three great passage graves making up the cemetery in the bend of the Boyne, and was far better known internationally before Dr Eogan began his spectacular excavations at Knowth. Its burial chamber had been known in modern times since 1699 at least, when its entrance was uncovered by men taking away material for road-building. The flat-topped mound is about the same size as Knowth, between eleven and thirteen metres high, with a diameter that varies between 79 and 85 metres, giving it a distinctly heart-shaped effect. The kerb-stones at Newgrange are also decorated, though not as profusely as those at Knowth. But to make up for this, it has what is probably the most magnificently decorated stone of any passage grave in Europe. This is the stone which lies in front of the entrance to the passage. Spirals and lozenges, pocked out as at Knowth, form a beautifully asymmetrical composition on either side of a line running vertically down the centre of the stone which, like the one on the stone outside the 1967 tomb at Knowth, must have marked the entrance to the passage leading to the tomb. The passage and chamber at New-grange closely resemble the eastern (1968) tomb at Knowth in the method of construction: the passage is roofed with lintels and rises as it approaches the chamber, which has a soaring corbelled roof of almost exactly similar dimensions to that at Knowth. The walls and some of the roof-stones of the chamber are marvellously decorated in much the same style, and the richness of the ornamentation in the right-hand (eastern) burial niche, together with the presence of a double stone basin there, show that, as at Knowth, it was obviously regarded as being of special importance.

Since they were first erected thousands of years ago, the upright stones supporting the roof of the passage tended to fall inwards under the weight of the mound which they had to bear. With the increase in the number of visitors to the tomb in the late 1950s and

This great spiral-decorated stone stands sentinel in front of the tomb at Newgrange. Beside the entrance is the movable stone door, and above it can be seen the recently-restored 'roof-box'.

early 1960s, a meeting was convened by the Irish Tourist Board, at which it was decided to straighten the stones to allow easier and safer access to the chamber. This necessitated removing the mound above the passage and encasing the passage in concrete in order to prevent the stones from buckling in the same way again. Professor M. J. O'Kelly of University College, Cork, volunteered to undertake the task, and this rescue operation has enabled him to carry out excavations on the chamber and on other parts of the site every year since he started in 1962. The removal of the hundreds of river-rounded stones from the cairn above the passage yielded considerable information about the constructional intelligence, which would otherwise not have been revealed, of the passage-grave builders. On the upper face of the stones forming the corbelling of the chamber and the roof of the passage, Professor O'Kelly found that narrow channels had been pecked into the surface. These channels apparently served to drain off any rainwater which might seep down through the top of the mound on to the stones above the chamber, and the dryness of the burial chamber to this day is proof of the soundness of the builders' techniques. Furthermore, the stones of the corbelled roof could now clearly be seen to slant downwards, away from the chamber; and this served the dual purpose of draining off the rain and of preventing the stones from falling into the chamber. Stripping the mound also gave an indication of the date of its construction. Samples of some of the soil packed into the spaces between the roof-stones of the passage produced two radiocarbon dates of around 2500 BC. This date suggests that Newgrange was built many centuries after the passage graves in Brittany. During his excavations, Professor O'Kelly naturally also searched the mound carefully for traces of a second tomb chamber like that at Knowth, but although he has removed a considerable amount of stone from that part of the mound which lies diametrically opposite to the entrance to the known chamber, he has been unable to find anything. However, there is still a vast amount of the mound at Newgrange which he has not yet had time to uncover, and future efforts may still be crowned with success.

The replacement of the stones of the roof of the passage at Newgrange has led to one intriguing piece of knowledge which demonstrates more clearly than anything else that the passage-grave builders were far from being the primitive cave-man savages of popular legend, but rather that they were an intellectually sophisticated people capable of producing as accurate a calendar as their near contemporaries, the pyramid builders in Egypt. A few feet above the entrance to the passage there was a stone which bore ornamentation of conjoined criss-crossed rectangles. There was an open space between it and the capstones of the passage below forming a sort of roof-box, and a gap in the capstones themselves; and ever since the nineteenth century, when this roof-box had first been noticed, it had been thought that it had been a repository for food which could be dropped down through the gap in the capstones as sustenance for the dead in the after-life. But as a result of clearing out the roof-box and putting the capstones back in their proper position, and because of acute observation on the part of Professor O'Kelly, it became apparent that this theory would have to be scrapped in favour of a much more ingenious explanation.

On Midwinter Day in 1969 (December 21) and on exactly the same day a year later, Professor O'Kelly spent the early morning waiting in the burial chamber for the sun to rise, in order to test out a hunch he had. When the sun began to lift over the eastern horizon, he watched in the burial chamber as a narrow beam of sunlight came through the roof-box and the gap in the capstones and crept its way briefly into the innermost recesses of the chamber. The

OPPOSITE
After excavation, the passage to the tomb at Newgrange was encased in concrete to prevent the uprights being buckled in future by the weight of the stones of the mound.

slender beam reached the hindmost burial niche at 9.58 a.m., and shone there until 10.15 a.m., when it disappeared as quickly and as quietly as it had come. Those seventeen minutes and a few more on the days immediately before and after December 21, are the only part of the year in which the sun's rays can reach the chamber at Newgrange, and the only way they can get in is through the roof-box. As Newgrange was built on top of a hill, the passage leading from the edge of the mound towards its centre had to go uphill; and so the horizontal rays of the sun could not reach all the way up the long slope of the passage. The only possible architectural solution was to pierce a hole above the entrance to the passage, to allow the sunlight to enter at a sufficiently high level to enable it to reach the back of the tomb—and this apparently had been what the original builders had done. They had constructed the roof-box above the entrance to the passage just in order to allow the sun into the tomb for a few brief minutes every year. But the very fact that the passage-grave builders put all their ingenuity to work in allowing the sun to do so, shows just how significant an occasion it must have been to them. It was a ritual method of marking the shortest day of the year—an important day in the agricultural calendar, for the farmers would know that a certain number of days after this event it would be time to start sowing the crops which would help sustain the community for the coming year.

Professor O'Kelly's discovery about the use of the roof-box and the penetration of the sun into the chamber on the shortest day of the year also pointed to the fact that the builders of the tomb must have planned the tomb so carefully that the straight line leading from the back of the tomb to the centre of the roof-box would align with the spot on the horizon where the sun would rise only once a year—on December 21. The careful orientation of the tomb and passage at Newgrange presupposes that their builders must have had some knowledge of astronomy and the movements of the sun, and possibly also the moon. It is not without significance that the mound at Newgrange is sited off-centre within a circle of large and rough-hewn standing stones of which only twelve out of an estimated original total of thirty-five survive. Smaller but similar stone circles were common in the Bronze Age, and the theory has become more and more generally accepted that the purpose of these later stone circles was to make astronomical and, therefore, calendar observations from them. If we push the Bronze Age evidence back into the Stone Age at Newgrange, we could—without too great a

stretch of the imagination—see the stone circle surrounding the great mound at Newgrange as an early astronomical observatory. The fact that the mound itself, sited on the highest point of the hill, was placed off-centre within the stone circle suggests that the two may not have been built at the same time, but at present we cannot say with certainty which is the older construction. It is quite conceivable, however, that the stone circle is the older, and that the mound builders may have based the orientation of their tomb on solar observations which had already been made in the circle.

But who was meant to see the sun coming into the burial chamber at Newgrange on the shortest day of the year? Was it intended only for the dead, who were immured in the tomb by the large stone door across the entrance? Or did the living push aside the door and enter the tomb each year when the sun was at its lowest, to experience those few short minutes when its slender rays illuminated the sacred precinct? Or could it be that Newgrange and Knowth were not primarily tombs, but rather ritual centres of the community, where the burial of the dead and the reckoning of the year's shortest day were only a part of the rites which took place there, and which necessitated occasional access to the chamber?

3

The Miners of Metal: the Earlier Bronze Age

Almost a decade before he started excavating at Newgrange, Professor O'Kelly had discovered almost by chance a method of cooking which had been used in the Bronze Age. When he was excavating a round house of the Early Christian period at Bally-vourney, Co. Cork, in 1953, his attention had been drawn to two other sites which, on first inspection, he took to be two other houses of the same type and period. One of these certainly suggested the outlines of a round house buried under the soil; it was a saucer-like depression surrounded by a circle of stone slabs, the tops of which were just visible above the ground surface. But when he excavated, he found something entirely different. The stones proved to be friable and burnt, and the depression turned out to be a timber-lined cooking-trough which had once contained water. Other features he discovered included two separate hearths, and a pit with walls and floor lined with stones. Professor O'Kelly gradually came to the conclusion that what he had stumbled upon was not an Early Christian house at all, but a much older cooking-site of the type known in Irish folk tradition as *Fulacht Fian* or *Fulacht Fiadh*—a 'cooking-site of the Fianna' (a legendary group of early Irish mercenaries) or 'of meat'.

The trough was wedge-shaped, measuring about 1·75 by 1 metre, and it had originally been 50 cms deep. The timbers on three sides had been lined on the outside with turf. Water seeped in continually through the timbers from the surrounding bog, and the site had obviously been deliberately chosen to give the trough a constant supply of water. There was a hearth near each end of the trough; one hearth, which seemed to have been in use at the same time as the trough, had three separate layers of ash; the other had seven fire-layers. If each layer of ash represented one day's cooking, then the minimum occupation of the site was ten days, but of course the site may not have been used every day.

The stone-lined pit was much larger than the timber-lined trough, and measured just under two metres square and was about 60 cms deep. It had been dug on slightly higher ground than the trough, and so remained dry. Beside it was found a layer of charcoal which looked as if it had been shovelled straight out of the pit. As many of the stones had a burned appearance, it was thought at first that this was some kind of roasting oven.

Nearby lay the remains of a small oval-shaped wooden hut that had been made of ten wooden posts sloping inwards and one placed upright in the centre. Inside it was a rectangular setting of stakes, which may have held a bed or a 'butcher's block'; and two vertical posts near the eastern side of the hut were tentatively interpreted as a possible rack on which the meat had been hung. Around the whole site was a dump of broken and burnt stone, all of it local sandstone of varying sizes. There were very few artefacts found— a spindle whorl and some stone discs—and nothing that could be used as evidence for dating. But a charcoal sample taken from a similar site excavated by Professor O'Kelly shortly afterwards at Killeens, also in Co. Cork, gave two radiocarbon dates suggesting that Killeens was being used around the eighteenth century BC, and therefore in the Earlier Bronze Age.

The type of cooking practised on the site at Ballyvourney seemed to correspond with that used by the Fianna, described around 1635 by Geoffrey Keating in his *History of Ireland*. Keating relates:

'They (the Fianna) only took one meal in twenty-four hours, and that was in the afternoon. And it was their custom to send their attendants with whatever they had killed in the morning's hunt to an appointed hill, having wood and moorland in the neighbourhood, and to kindle raging fires thereon, and put into them a large number of emery stones; and to dig two pits in the yellow clay of the moorland, and put some of the meat on spits to roast before the fire; and to bind another portion of it with *sugáns* (straw ropes) in dry bundles, and set it to boil in the larger of the two pits, and keep plying them with stones that were in the fire, making them seethe often till they were cooked. And these fires were so large that their sites are today in Ireland burnt to black-

The cooked meat, still wrapped in straw, is taken from the boiling water in the cooking experiment carried out at a *Fulacht Fiadh* at Ballyvourney.

ness, and these are now called *Fulacht Fian* by the peasantry.'

Professor O'Kelly then decided upon a culinary experiment, in which he used the method described by Keating to test the kind of cooking that might have taken place at this nomadic, seasonal cooking-site at Ballyvourney. He discovered that two inexperienced men could build the whole site in twenty hours—hut, cooking-trough, hearth and stone-lined pit—and he suggested that those practised in the art could probably have done it in half that time.

The reconstructed trough could hold 455 litres of water; but because it was a dry season, not enough water seeped in on its own, and extra water had to be added from a nearby stream. The hearth was set with a layer of stones taken from nearby outcrops of sandstone, then fuel was added and a second layer of stones piled on top. The fire was lit, and after about an hour, red-hot stones were available from both top and bottom layers. The stones were then

41

thrown into the water of the cooking-trough with a wooden shovel, and by this method of immersion heating the water was brought to the boil in half an hour or so. From then on, only a few more stones thrown in at intervals were needed to keep it boiling. Professor O'Kelly then took a ten-pound leg of mutton which he wrapped in a covering of clean straw and tied with the *sugáns* (straw ropes). Using the time-hallowed formula of 'twenty minutes to the pound and twenty minutes over', he left the wrapped joint in the boiling water for three hours and forty minutes. The water turned opaque, and the surface was covered with a scum of globules of fat and ashes, but the meat itself was kept free of contamination by the straw covering. On removal of the straw, the meat was found to be cooked through and through. 'Very tasty' was the final verdict. So the method of cooking described by Keating proved to have been the same as that used possibly as many as three thousand years earlier at Ballyvourney, showing a remarkable continuity in Irish tradition!

But what of the stone-lined pit? In Keating's *History of Ireland*, the Fianna had put it to special use, as a bath:

'As to the Fianna, when they assembled on the hill on which the fire was, each of them stripped off, and tied his shirt round his waist; and they ranged themselves around the second pit, bathing their hair and washing their limbs . . . and after this they took their meal; and when they had taken their meal, they proceeded to build their hunting tents, and so prepared themselves for sleep.'

Professor O'Kelly decided to see if the stone-lined pit could have been used not as a bath but as a roasting oven. He built a fire in the pit itself to heat the stone slabs that lined the walls, then brushed out the ashes and put in another ten-pound leg of mutton, which he covered with stones from the hearth. He roasted the mutton in this way for the prescribed three hours and forty minutes, changing the stones only seven times to keep the temperature up. Once again, the meat tasted excellent; but because of the size of the pit, the stone lining of the sides had very little effect on the cooking—all the 'work' was done by the heated stones applied from the hearth. So perhaps, after all, the literary traditions were right, and the stone-lined pit was not a roasting oven after all, but nothing more nor less than an early Irish bath-tub.

Professor O'Kelly's excavations around the base of the mound at

Newgrange produced among other things a number of animal bones which show what kind of meat was cooked by people in Ireland at the beginning of the Earlier Bronze Age—the period when the cooking pits were probably in use. Beef was the most popular item on the menu, but herds of pigs, sheep and goats were also destined for consumption. Horses were used for riding, and possibly also for food as well.

But these people whose traces Professor O'Kelly had found around the base of the burial mound at Newgrange were not the same as those who had built it, and they lived about five centuries later. They belonged to a new race, whom archaeologists label as the Beaker people. They are so called after the pots they used, which resemble the modern quaffing vessels of that name. This Beaker pottery makes its appearance in the archaeological record in many parts of Europe in the years shortly before and after 2000 BC. The origin of the people who made this pottery is shrouded in mystery, but one theory is that they spread westwards from eastern and central Europe. Their diffusion was so rapid, and covered such a vast area, that it can best be explained by the suggestion that they were among Europe's earliest horsemen.

It was around 2100 BC that the Beaker people arrived at New-grange. By that time, the entrance to the tomb and to the roof-box had already been obscured and forgotten, and the material of the mound had slipped down the slope and covered the kerb-stones. It was on top of this slip that the Beaker Folk squatted. To judge by the traces they left behind on and around the debris of the mound, they were technologically more advanced than the passage-grave people; a flat bronze axe which was found in the Beaker settlement shows that they were already metal users. Despite this, the most common implements found on the site were made of the older-established flint, and included scrapers, arrowheads and polished disc knives. Besides fragments of decorated Beaker pottery, and a four-footed bowl of a type more commonly found in central Europe, Professor O'Kelly discovered an ovoid hammer stone with hour-glass perforation. Almost nothing remains of the houses or huts in which these people lived, apart from hearths and an occasional post-hole.

Strange as it may seem, scarcely any Beaker pottery was known from Ireland half a century ago, and it is only with the excavations within the last twenty-five years—such as that at Newgrange—that it has become apparent how strong the new wave of Beaker

Four-footed bowl from Newgrange made by the Beaker Folk.

immigrants must have been in Ireland. The discovery of an ever-increasing amount of Beaker pottery, particularly in the northern half of the country, is beginning to indicate the tremendous contribution which these people made to the subsequent population of the country; as is suggested in the next chapter, they may even have been responsible for the introduction of a new language which could be the ancestor of the Irish language still spoken in the country to this day. Later generations of their progeny were probably involved in the making of Food Vessels, a very decorative form of pottery which was the most popular of all gravegoods deposited with the dead during the Earlier Bronze Age.

Outside Ireland, the Beaker people buried their dead in single-graves. In Ireland, they occasionally continued to use the megalithic tombs which had been built shortly before their arrival, which shows how easily they adapted themselves to local conditions, but so far no Beaker pottery has been found in a single-grave in Ireland. Instead, we find the burials of the Earlier Bronze Age in Ireland often accompanied by Food Vessels and Urns; they were usually isolated, but sometimes they formed cemeteries. A typically Irish form of cemetery was the so-called 'multiple cist cairn'. This was a mound, smaller than that covering a passage grave, and containing a primary burial and a number of secondary burials placed in stone-lined boxes called cists, which—unlike the passage graves—had no access to them once the capstone was put on the cist and it was covered with soil or stones. One such mound was excavated at Poulawack, Co. Clare, in 1934 by the same Harvard Archaeological Mission which re-excavated Kilgreany Cave, but in this instance under the direction of Professor Hugh Hencken. The mound was situated at the highest point of a flat-topped hill in the magnificently wild and rocky terrain of the Burren in Co. Clare, an area excellently suited to the winter pasturage of cattle. The mound or cairn, which consisted largely of stones, was about twenty metres in diameter and just over three metres high, and was found to contain the remains of no fewer than eighteen individuals. Within the cairn was a round wall, which was strengthened by a circular setting of stones just outside it. Outside this inner wall an adult male lay buried, surrounded by a number of upright stones; but this burial may have been older than the mound. Six burials were laid down before the mound was heaped over them. Two of them were placed side by side in the centre of the mound, and these were obviously the main interments. They were in two separately made but conjoined cists

Poulawack in the course of excavation. Behind the circular wall in the foreground stands one of the stone cists.

made of upright stones and covered by two capstones. They contained the scattered remains of four individuals—a man and a woman of middle age, a young woman aged about twenty-one, and an infant of a year old. They may well have belonged to the same family, and were possibly all interred together after they had been buried separately elsewhere immediately after death—there is no need to conclude that they had all died simultaneously. The burials show that life expectancy at the time cannot have been very high. Of the eighteen people buried in various parts of the mound at Poulawack, eight had died before reaching the age of fifteen, and of these, three had not lived for more than two or three years. Only two of the eighteen are likely to have been over thirty-five when they died. Very few finds came to light during the excavation, but one was a small sherd of Beaker pottery, suggesting that it was possibly the Beaker folk who built the mound.

At around the same time as the arrival of the Beaker people, the transition from the Stone to the Bronze Age took place, though there is as yet no conclusive proof that the two events were related to one another. The main technological change between the ages of stone and bronze was the introduction of the use of metal. This was at first copper and gold, and then at a later stage bronze. Gold was panned in rivers in Wicklow, and probably elsewhere as well, and this valuable material was used for the making of some exquisite ornaments which can now be seen in the National Museum of Ireland in Dublin; the collection of prehistoric gold there, indeed,

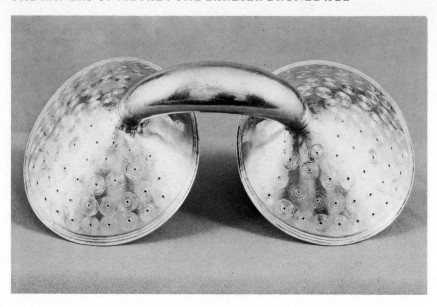

A heavy gold 'dress fastener' of about the eighth century BC, found near Clones, Co. Monaghan.

is only bettered in Europe by those in Athens and Budapest. The earliest of these gold ornaments were made of thin sheets of gold, and included small decorated discs and crescent-shaped chest ornaments called *lunulae*. Later in the Bronze Age, when larger supplies of gold became available, massive ornaments of solid gold were manufactured. Some of these expand at the ends like the mouth of a trumpet, but what their precise use was no one can say. Towards the end of the Bronze Age, other neck ornaments called gorgets show the heights of technical ingenuity which Bronze Age gold-smiths could achieve in Ireland.

Copper was normally used for the manufacture of implements and weapons. Ireland is probably the only country in western Europe which retains some of its Earlier Bronze Age copper mines intact. About twenty-five of these can be seen high up on the slopes of Mount Gabriel in West Cork. They were saved from destruction by being covered by the same blanket bog which had preserved the Neolithic ridges and furrows in Co. Mayo. It was only when the bog was cut to obtain fuel about a century ago that the mines were revealed in much the same state as they had been in the Earlier Bronze Age.

The mines are simple affairs. A passage about one metre or 1·30 metres wide and as little as 80 cms high at the entrance expands inwards and downwards into the mine proper. The total length of the passage and mine combined does not exceed ten metres. The area where the mining took place was rarely more than 1·60 metres high and five metres wide. The miners would have lighted fires in these cramped surroundings and waited until the rock heated; then they would have poured cold water on it, causing it to crack and split. This allowed them to remove the ore with the aid of mining mauls or hammers. The ore was then brought out into the fresh air and cobbed—that is, the ore was separated from the gangue or waste rock which surrounded it. In other parts of the world where such simple mining operations are known to have been carried on in modern times, it was always women who did the cobbing on what are known as cobbing floors. No cobbing floors were discovered at Mount Gabriel, although one might have expected to find them somewhere near the mouth of the mines.

Dr John Jackson and Dr Joseph Raftery of the National Museum of Ireland carried out a small excavation at Mount Gabriel in 1966. They cut a trial trench through a tip-heap outside the entrance to one of the mines, and found a number of mining mauls in the upper layers. These makeshift hammers had been made from cobbles which had been brought up from the nearby seashore. Some were designed to be hand-held, while others had a groove at the waist to accommodate a rope handle to increase the force of the blow. A charcoal sample from the excavation gave a radiocarbon date of

Reconstruction drawing of a metal workshop of the Later Bronze Age, around 700 BC.

A bronze dagger-blade of about 1500 BC. Its original handle, possibly of wood, has not survived.

1500 ± 120 BC, which places the mining activity firmly in the Earlier Bronze Age of Ireland.

The copper won from these mines was later used to make axes and daggers which developed as the Bronze Age proceeded. The simple flat axe, representing the earliest stage of development, was given upstanding sides or flanges so that it would not slip around in its wooden haft when it struck wood. Weapons were at first made with copper, but later they were almost invariably made of bronze, which was achieved by a mixture of ninety per cent copper and ten per cent tin. The earliest Bronze Age weapons were short daggers hafted with a wooden handle, and the changes which the blade went through in the course of the Bronze Age is the main criterion for the dating of these weapons. Shortly after 1400 BC it became possible to cast longer weapons, and the dirk or rapier emerged. Another curious implement much beloved in Ireland was the halberd, in which a copper or bronze blade was hafted at right angles to a long wooden handle. Many of the bronze weapons in Ireland were recovered from bogs and rivers. They were rarely buried with the dead, who seemed to have no need of them in the Otherworld—or at least, not as much as the living!

OPPOSITE
One of the niches of the burial chamber in Newgrange has a highly decorated capstone as well as two ritual stone basins placed one above the other.

4

The Fort Builders: the Later Bronze Age and the Earlier Iron Age

After the start of the Later Bronze Age in Ireland around 1200 BC, a whole new range of bronze implements and weapons such as socketed axe-heads and swords were introduced. The bronze industry which produced these flourished for many hundreds of years, and reached its zenith in the eighth century BC when sheet-bronze was used to great effect in the manufacture of splendid cauldrons, buckets, shields and trumpets. At the same time, gold-smiths were active particularly in the Lower Shannon area producing finely-worked gold ornaments. But no one can say for certain how long this Later Bronze Age metal industry survived. Some arch-aeologists think that the introduction of iron around the sixth century BC put an end to the Bronze Age industry, while others believe that bronze remained the main metal used in Ireland until the third century BC. This difference of opinion has arisen largely because of the lack of characteristic material which could be dated to those crucial centuries from 600 to 200 BC and which could thereby help in solving the problem. But some light has recently been shed on these dark years by the excavation of sites that yielded radiocarbon dates which fall within this period.

These dates have been won from hill-forts, large enclosures on hill-tops surrounded by a bank and ditch. In some cases the ditch runs unexpectedly inside the bank instead of outside it, and this fact, combined with the practical difficulty of defending a wall hundreds of metres long, suggests that some at least of these enclosures were not fortifications but some form of ritual centres. Until recently these hill-forts were considered to belong to the Iron Age and were dated to some time after 300 BC. But recent excava-

From the National Museum of Ireland: (*above*) golden earrings of the Earlier Bronze Age period around 1200 BC, and (*below*) Later Bronze Age spiral bracelet (*right*), gold-plated lead ring (*left*) and pendant (*centre*) with a quizzical stylisation of the human face.

49

At Navan Fort, Dudley Waterman unravelled the foundation trenches of eight successive round houses, and the holes of four concentric circles of posts.

tions have shown that while they were certainly used in the Iron Age, human activity within them goes back at least as far as the seventh century BC, and thus to a period practically contemporary with the great sheet-metal industry which represents the finest achievement of the Later Bronze Age. Some of these excavated sites have produced in their interiors a bewildering number of round enclosures marked by shallow trenches, which were frequently renewed on almost the same spot.

One of the most notable examples is Navan Fort, situated near the town of Armagh, where an area eighteen acres in extent was surrounded by a bank with the ditch inside it. Within the fort was a mound which was excavated by Dudley Waterman of the Archaeological Survey of Northern Ireland. Under the mound he found the remains of a round house carbon-dated to around 680 BC, and sited in an enclosure with a diameter of 36 metres. The house—if such it really was—was renewed eight times in much the same form on almost exactly the same site in the course of the following three or four centuries, until the layout was changed around 400 BC when three further round houses were built on another part of the same site. Some time later, the whole complex underwent a complete change. Over the area of the original house enclosure a massive circular structure of timber was built, with a diameter of about 43 metres. The outer wall of this structure consisted of upright timbers four metres apart and joined by horizontal planks. Within it there were four concentric rings of post-holes in which upright posts had once been embedded, and in the centre of the whole structure there was one post-hole more

At the centre of the concentric circles of wooden posts under the mound at Navan Fort, a ramp led down to this stump, which must have had a special importance for its makers.

massive than the rest. It retained a wooden stump which must have had some sacred significance. It is not known if this structure was ever roofed. The most extraordinary thing about it was that while it was still standing, it was covered over by a mound of stone, turf and soil which, when Waterman excavated it, showed traces of what had once been the wooden uprights within it. The timber of the outer wall had been destroyed by fire around 265 BC. This structure, to have been preserved by being encased in the mound and possibly intentionally burned on the outside, must have had some great ceremonial purpose now beyond our ken, and it certainly suggests that in its last stage of use, the hill-fort in which it stood must have been a ritual site of prime importance. The question remains open as to whether the houses which preceded it on the site were simply dwelling places, or whether these oft-renewed buildings were constructed for some more lofty purpose. It is unfortunate also that no evidence has yet been revealed to connect the building activity within the enclosure with the building of the wall and ditch, so that we cannot yet say at what stage the bank was constructed.

Both bronze and iron were used by the inhabitants of Navan Fort, but their remains are so sparse that we cannot yet say whether one succeeded the other as the dominant material, or whether both were used to an equal extent at the same time. But the discovery of a bronze workshop in another hill-fort of much the same date as the Navan Fort building now shows how important bronze was for the inhabitants of hill-forts. This workshop came to light during the excavations which have been carried out since 1969 at Rathgall in the Wicklow Hills by Barry Raftery, a lecturer in archaeology in University College, Dublin. In the centre of this hill-fort Barry Raftery found a round house, fifteen metres in diameter, that was surrounded by a V-sectioned ditch. Outside the eastern section of this ditch, he found a thick deposit of black organic material which was associated with a rectangular, black burnt layer (probably the remains of a hearth), as well as an area of cobbling and a number of post-holes which may have formed part of a large timber structure. As the finds showed, this timber building was no ordinary dwelling house; it turned out to be the first Later Bronze Age workshop yet located in Ireland. More than four hundred fragments of clay moulds were discovered in the western part of the building near the supposed hearth and the cobbling. The broken moulds, made of fine grey clay, had been used to cast swords, spearheads and also, probably, socketed axes and gouges or chisels. One

Aerial photo of the Rathgall hill-fort, showing the apparently medieval stone wall encircling the earlier occupation area. Half of the bedding trench of the circular house can be seen in the centre of the fort.

fragment of mould still retained a broken blade which had been discarded because it had fused with the clay of the mould. Another two or three hundred mould fragments were found some distance away from the main workshop, showing the considerable extent of the bronze-working area. Gold may also have been worked in the compound, as five gold pieces came to light during the course of the excavation, one of them a gold penannular ring normally called 'ring money'. It will be remembered that streams not far distant in the Wicklow Hills were some of the most prolific sources of gold in prehistoric Ireland.

Radiocarbon dates from Rathgall suggest that the Later Bronze Age occupation may have started as early as 980 BC and continued to 265 BC, but it has so far proved impossible to obtain an exact radiocarbon dating for the bronze workshop. Barry Raftery thinks that it is likely to have been in production during the seventh or sixth century BC, and if we take into consideration the continuity of use of the site of Navan Fort from the seventh to the third century BC, we could surmise not only that bronze was the most important metal of the early occupiers of hill-forts but also that it might have remained so until possibly as late as the third century BC.

Rathgall has also distinguished itself by producing the first grave and funeral pyre which can be reliably dated to the Later Bronze Age in Ireland. The custom of burying gravegoods with the dead had petered out in Ireland around 1300 BC, and people buried during the ensuing thousand years were presumably interred without any trappings, which is obviously why it had been difficult until recently to recognise and identify any graves from the Later Bronze Age. But in an elaborate burial complex contemporary with the Later Bronze Age occupation at Rathgall, Barry Raftery found the grave of an adult whose body had been burned before its remains were buried in a small circular pit. There were no accompanying gravegoods, but the pit had been dug into a red, heavily burnt area in which patches of black sooty material occurred. These contained splinters of human bone and must undoubtedly represent the remnants of a funeral pyre. Had it not been for the fortunate circumstance that the individual cremated at Rathgall had been buried in an unmistakeably Later Bronze Age context, it would have been impossible to date the burial to this period at all.

Over the Later Bronze Age layer at Rathgall traces of Iron Age occupation were found. They included a bronze strap-tag dating from the first few centuries after Christ, and also large quantities of iron slag found beside a pit containing alternating layers of pure charcoal and some sandy grey material. In 1974 a carbon date relating to this Iron Age activity gave a reading of AD 265, which suggests that a considerable time must have elapsed before iron-working was practised on the same site where earlier the bronze workshop had been active.

Only about fifty hill-forts are known in Ireland. In contrast, what at first sight might seem like their little brothers, the ring-forts, are much more numerous, totalling probably more than 30,000. The ring-fort, known in Irish as *rath*, is indeed probably the most common and widespread field monument in the country. A ring-fort consisted of a house or group of houses inside a circular area, about an acre in extent, which was enclosed by an earthen bank and ditch, the former sometimes topped by a palisade of wood. The word 'fort' is perhaps a misnomer, for the ring-fort was not a military stronghold but merely a normal homestead sheltered by a wall to keep livestock in and marauders out. Where ring-forts can be dated they have proved to have been built largely in the Early Christian

Fragments of clay moulds used to cast spearheads found at Rathgall.

period, that is, after AD 400, and some are even known to have been in use as late as the seventeenth century. Although it has been claimed, though not necessarily generally accepted, that the ring-fort may have its origins in the Late Stone Age, two examples at least were presumably built during the Early Iron Age. One of these is the Rath of the Synods on the Hill of Tara which will be discussed in the next chapter. The other is the Rath of Feerwore (Fort of the Big Men) in Co. Galway, which was excavated by Barry Raftery's father, Joseph Raftery, in 1938. Dr Raftery has for long been the Curator of Irish Antiquities in the National Museum of Ireland in Dublin, and the most experienced worker in the field of Iron Age studies in Ireland. In the rath he was able to distinguish four phases of occupation, the first two of which proved to be older than the construction of the fort's bank and ditch. Belonging to one or other of these early phases were a bronze fibula or brooch dating from around the first century BC, and a small glass bead. But a pagan burial in a stone setting ascribed to one of the last two phases of occupation on the site showed that the bank and ditch, which belonged to the third phase, must have been built before the coming of Christianity in the fifth century AD, and therefore during the Early Iron Age.

Outside the Rath of Feerwore there once stood a very significant stone now known as the Turoe Stone, which got its name from the house to which it was removed many years ago. What had attracted Dr Raftery to the site originally had been the prospect of establishing a connection between the rath and the stone, but this he was unfortunately unable to do. The Turoe Stone is about one metre high, and its upper part is decorated in handsome curvilinear patterns which are typical of the work of Celtic craftsmen in Ireland, Britain and continental Europe. Celtic art, to which this decoration on the Turoe Stone belongs, evolved in central Europe in the fifth century BC, and is commonly known as the 'La Tène style' after a site in Switzerland where it was first identified and defined in the last century. The name La Tène indeed is often applied in general to that period of the Iron Age covering the fifth to the first centuries BC. The La Tène style is a collective name for a number of individual art-styles, of which that found on the Turoe Stone is described as the Waldalgesheim style, called after a place in Germany where objects decorated in this style were found. The Waldalgesheim style developed in central Europe sometime towards the end of the fourth century BC and this therefore provided the earliest possible date for

The Turoe Stone.

the carving of the Turoe Stone. But because it may have taken up to a century for this style to have reached Ireland, the Turoe Stone is likely to date from some little time after 300 BC and may even be contemporary with the first or second phase of the Rath of Feerwore. The decoration on the Turoe Stone stands at the centre of a controversy concerning the route or routes by which La Tène art (and the Celts in the La Tène period) came to Ireland. Some art historians feel that it came via Brittany where stones bearing related decoration are known, while others think that it represents a more 'insular' variant of the style which may have developed in Britain from impulses received from central Europe.

Certainly this Waldalgesheim style was the inspiration of much Celtic decoration produced by Irish craftsmen in the period after

300 BC. It was also used to stunning effect on gold objects, one of the best known of which is a gold collar found at Broighter in Co. Derry together with a number of other gold objects. These comprised a necklace of three plaited chains and another of only one plaited chain; one complete and one fragmentary torque (neck-ring) of spirally twisted gold with thinner wire around it; a hemispherical bowl with attachment loops and, finally, a boat with a mast and mast-yard, eight seats, fourteen oars for rowing and one for steering. The gold with which these fine objects were made contains platinum, a substance not known to exist in Ireland, so that the gold, worked or unworked, must have been imported into Ireland. Platinum is known from the Upper Rhine valley, but recent work on gold analyses suggests that platinum in gold could also have originated in England. In view of the possible English origin of the gold from the Broighter hoard, it is interesting to digress for a moment to recall the history of this hoard since its discovery, as it was the cause of a celebrated tug of war between Ireland and England around the turn of the century.

Two ploughmen turned up the hoard in a field at Broighter near Lough Foyle in 1896, and were given a reward of five pounds by their master, a man named Gibson, when they brought the gold objects to him. Gibson sold them to a dealer in Belfast who in turn passed them on to Robert Day, who was Ireland's foremost private collector of antiquities at the time. Day realised that the discovery was of no ordinary significance and brought it to the notice of the Society of Antiquaries of London. In January 1897 Arthur Evans— the future excavator of Knossos—published a paper on the find for the Society, and thus became the first person to announce to the public the existence of the Broighter find and to describe what it contained.

When news of Evans's paper reached Dublin, the Royal Irish Academy was stirred to action and asked the British Treasury to declare the hoard Treasure Trove; the Academy normally acted for the British Treasury on such matters in Ireland, and assumed that the Treasury would reciprocate and declare the Broighter find Treasure Trove in due course. But nothing was done; and meanwhile the British Museum, realising that the hoard contained far finer pieces of Celtic gold than anything else in its collection, bought the hoard from Robert Day for six hundred pounds, and took possession of it in May 1897. All this was done without the knowledge of the Royal Irish Academy. When the news eventually broke

The gold torque from the Broighter hoard is decorated with typically Celtic swirling ornament and has a sophisticated closing mechanism.

in the following year, John Redmond, the Irish parliamentarian and leading Home Ruler, introduced a Private Member's Bill in Westminster to enable the British Museum to hand over any of its collection to the recently opened National Museum in Dublin. But objections were raised to the Bill because it was too wide in its scope, and it was blocked. Despite this, further questions were asked in Parliament about the return of the Broighter find to Dublin. The British Museum replied that it was not legally empowered to alienate any of the objects in its possession, even though at this stage Robert Day offered to buy back the hoard at its original sale price. As there had recently been a similar case, in which the British Museum had acquired a valuable Scottish antiquity, the Glenlyon Brooch, which many a proud Scot felt should have remained north of the Border, a Parliamentary Commission was set up to look into the matter of whether the British Museum could hand over some of the items in its collection to the Dublin or Edinburgh Museums. The Commission recommended that the British Museum should relax its regulations slightly in exceptional cases, but despite this, the Broighter hoard remained in London.

The Royal Irish Academy, backed up by George Coffey, the Dublin Museum's energetic and scholarly Curator, refused to give up the fight. It culminated in June 1903 in a celebrated court case: the Attorney-General *versus* the Trustees of the British Museum, with the great Irish pleader Edward Carson (then Solicitor-General for England) arguing the case for the Attorney-General. Carson maintained that the Broighter find was Treasure Trove, which was defined as bullion (gold or silver) which had been lost or concealed by an unknown owner with the intention of recovering it at some later date. Under those circumstances, the hoard is deemed to belong to the Crown, which shall reward the finder appropriately. If, however, the original owner had thrown it away or had lost it casually by letting it drop, for instance, into the sea, without having any intention of recovering it, it is deemed to belong to the owner of the land on which it is found. The criterion for Treasure Trove, therefore, is that it was concealed with the intention of recovery, but never actually recovered by the owner, and in the court case Carson maintained that this criterion was fulfilled in the case of the Broighter treasure. The Trustees of the British Museum, on the other hand, maintained that the objects had been thrown away without any intention of recovery, and advanced two arguments in support of their claim to keep them. The first was that the place where the gold objects had been found had been under the sea at the time they were discarded; their second argument was that the objects had in fact been part of a votive offering to gain the favour of some deity or deities unknown, and that therefore the people who had made the offering clearly had no intention of trying to recover the objects.

However, Justice Farwell, who presided over the case, said in his judgement that there was no evidence to suggest that the sea had covered the find-spot in question during the life-span of the objects; nor, he said, was there any evidence to suggest that votive offerings had ever been made in Europe since the Bronze Age, and these objects were clearly later than the Bronze Age. 'There is no case known of a votive offering anywhere of a ship coupled with other miscellaneous articles,' he stated, 'and there is no case on record of any votive offering having been made in Ireland at any time.' As a result of Justice Farwell's findings, the Broighter hoard was declared Treasure Trove and was ordered to be handed over to the Crown. Shortly afterwards, King Edward VII decreed that the objects should be returned to Ireland and be given to the Royal Irish Academy, which displayed them in the National Museum of Ireland in Dublin, where they still form part of the Museum's dazzling exhibition of prehistoric gold.

We find that the Celtic art style used in the decoration of the Broighter gold collar and the Turoe Stone is also encountered on bronze objects of a similar date found in Ireland, including fibulae or brooches, horse-bits, spear-butts and discs. But, strange to say, these bronze objects are without any exact parallels outside the country, and belong to types only found in Ireland. It would thus seem that it was only the art style and not the types of objects which had been introduced into Ireland from outside during the Iron Age. This is most likely to have happened through the agency of a handful of craftsmen coming from Britain or the Continent. It is also quite likely that a knowledge of iron and the weapons which were made with it were introduced into Ireland by Celtic chieftains who came from Britain. If that is so, we could imagine Ireland to have been populated in the Iron Age largely by the descendants of those Bronze Age people who had built that strange timber structure in Navan Fort and had a bronze workshop at Rathgall, but who were intruded upon by small bands of iron-using Celtic chieftains who may have been accompanied by Celtic craftsmen who manufactured objects of Irish type but decorated them in an art style which they had brought with them from Britain or ultimately from the Continent.

If we are drawing the picture of Iron Age Ireland correctly, we must then ask ourselves the question, when did the Celts come to Ireland and can these iron-wielding chieftains alone be made responsible for having made the country so entirely Celtic in its language, laws and institutions as it was at the beginning of the historic era in the fifth century AD? Many linguists consider that the Celts first came to Ireland during the Iron Age. Some Celts undoubtedly did arrive during that period, but were they the first and did they come in sufficient numbers to celticise the country entirely? The Irishness of the bronze objects decorated in the La Tène art style, and the paucity of iron as well as the comparative lack of fortifications in Ireland datable to the last few centuries BC would scarcely argue in favour of any large-scale invasion of the country at the time, and the Romans would surely have reported a big Celtic invasion of Ireland if it had taken place after they had occupied Britain in the first century AD.

If it seems unlikely from the archaeological evidence that the country was made entirely Celtic during the Iron Age, what other alternatives exist? Could those who occupied the hill-forts in the seventh century BC have been the first Celts in Ireland, or could these have been other people who used swords of so-called Hallstatt type which were based on continental prototypes and were introduced into Ireland in the seventh century BC? It is quite conceivable that they too could have been Celts, but if they were the first to have come to Ireland, we would have to take the rise of apparently ritual centres such as Navan Fort or the new products of

This bronze sword of the Late Bronze Age, manufactured around the eighth—seventh centuries BC, would originally have had a bone grip.

a bronze industry as the major criteria for a new influx of people, and this evidence can scarcely be said to be conclusive. But the tradition of burying the dead without gravegoods which persisted from about 1300 BC down to the Iron Age, and the continuity in the type of *Fulacht Fiadh* cooking-site lasting (as we saw in the last chapter) from the Earlier Bronze Age at Ballyvourney down to the seventeenth century AD, together with the largely native character of the bronze industry practised in the hill-forts, suggests that we might have to look further back in time for the coming to Ireland of the ancestors of those who spoke Celtic at the beginning of the historic period, without denying the likelihood of waves of Celtic-speaking peoples having come to Ireland during the Later Bronze Age and the Early Iron Age. When we do go back beyond the Later Bronze Age and search for evidence of a likely invasion, then we are most likely to find it in the Earlier Bronze Age, when the custom of single-burial we find spreading so rapidly and widely over the country during the first half of the second millennium BC stands in such obvious contrast to the communal burial practised by the builders of the Stone Age megalithic tombs that it can only be explained by a large-scale immigration of new peoples. The pottery we find buried in these single-graves largely consists of Food Vessels which are considered to have developed from the Beaker pottery made by those Beaker Folk whom we saw coming to Ireland around 2000 BC and squatting at the base of the great passage-grave mound at Newgrange. In the future, it may be upon these Beaker Folk and their immediate descendants that we will have to call when we are asked to answer the question as to when the earliest ancestors of the Celts we know from the historic period came to Ireland, even though it may have been some form of undifferentiated Indo-European language rather than a fully developed Celtic tongue that they spoke at the time.

5

Monks and Laymen: the Early Christian Period

The Hill of Tara in Co. Meath has many powerful historical associations; but it is not the most obvious place to expect to find the Biblical Ark of the Covenant. But in 1899 an eccentric Englishman named Groome managed to convince himself that Tara was the proper place to look for it. Using a bizarre hotch-potch of Egyptian hieroglyphics, and indecipherable signs and patterns from prehistoric monuments, he had tracked the Ark as far as the coast of Palestine. There, however, the trail ran cold on him . . .

Later, quite by chance, he had picked up a little book in a second-hand bookshop in Charing Cross Road in London. This book contained similar weird signs and patterns; and after lengthy research in the British Museum, he decided that they bore a marked resemblance to certain markings on stones that had been found between Dundalk and Tara. Much encouraged by this providential coincidence, Mr Groome set off for Ireland, and there he got permission from three men who owned or leased the Rath of the Synods on top of Tara Hill to dig in pursuit of his quest.

Not surprisingly, Groome found no trace of the Ark; and when the three men saw that he was not finding traces of anything at all, they began to feel sorry for him. So they got hold of some Roman coins dating from the reign of the Emperor Constantine the Great early in the fourth century, and planted them carefully in the path of Groome's excavations—where, inevitably, he found them shortly afterwards. Groome now redoubled his efforts. The Office of Public Works was incensed at the way he was devastating the site and tried to stop him, only to discover that they had no jurisdiction to do so. Shortly afterwards two of the three men who had originally

Tara, official residence of the High Kings of ancient Ireland, still retains traces of ring-ditches and ring-forts such as the Rath of the Synods on the left.

granted permission to dig died untimely deaths, and the sole survivor, remembering a legend he had heard that whoever dug for the Ark would surely die, now put a stop to Mr Groome's activities, helped by the Royal Society of Antiquaries of Ireland. Groome, however, promptly got an intuition that his 'guide stone' had moved; he got 'indications' that the Ark must be buried on the opposite side of the road to where he had been digging. But when he was refused permission to continue his most unarchaeological spoliation there too, he packed his bags and returned to England. No more evidence of the Ark has since been found.

By coincidence, it turned out that the practical jokers had chosen coins of just the right period to plant in Mr Groome's path on the Rath of the Synods. Some fifty years later, as part of a large scale and still uncompleted scheme to excavate the whole Hill of Tara, the late Professor Seán P. Ó Ríordáin dug what was left intact of

OPPOSITE
The gold boat from Broighter is the earliest evidence for the use of sail in Irish waters.

the Rath of the Synods and came upon material to show that the site really had been used as a fort in four different phases from the first to the early fourth century AD. The Rath had three concentric rock-cut ditches which were separated by banks topped by wooden palisades. The site has been used for habitation, and also for ritual purposes as the seat of the priestly High Kings of Ireland. It was here, in AD 433, that the High King Laoghaire saw a light shining ten miles away on the Hill of Slane—a light kindled by St Patrick as a symbol of the new religion of Christianity which he was preaching. St Patrick failed to convert the High King himself, but he succeeded in converting practically the whole of the rest of his country to Christianity within his own lifetime—a feat made all the more remarkable in that it was achieved without the spilling of a single drop of martyr's blood.

The church which St Patrick founded in Ireland was organised at first on the basis of episcopal sees; but around the year 500 this system evolved into an organisation based on monasteries which were governed by abbots with ecclesiastical jurisdiction over the surrounding area. This monastic movement was extraordinarily vigorous throughout the sixth century, and the new foundations which it created became the great centres of culture in the following centuries, like Clonmacnoise in Co. Offaly. It was these foundations which furthered the use of writing and produced many great illuminated manuscripts which survive today, akin to the Book of Durrow in the seventh century and the Book of Kells in the eighth or ninth. Their scribes helped to write down and thereby preserve many of the old Celtic tales—including pagan lore—which would otherwise have been lost, and their workshops manufactured metal masterpieces like the Ardagh Chalice. The strange thing about these monasteries is that although we know something of their history and their artistic products which have been handed down from generation to generation, we know very little about what they must have looked like in the early years of their existence. Only a very few of the old Irish monasteries preserve above ground any traces prior to the ninth century; the physical remains of the earliest centuries—the really great centuries—of these monasteries have largely eluded archaeologists so far. Most of the dozen or so monasteries which have been excavated whole or in part have produced little or no evidence of existence during the sixth and seventh centuries, or else have produced none which can be reliably dated to this period. This is well exemplified at two separate sites, Nendrum and Reask, which

Incised animals on a stone tablet from Nendrum.

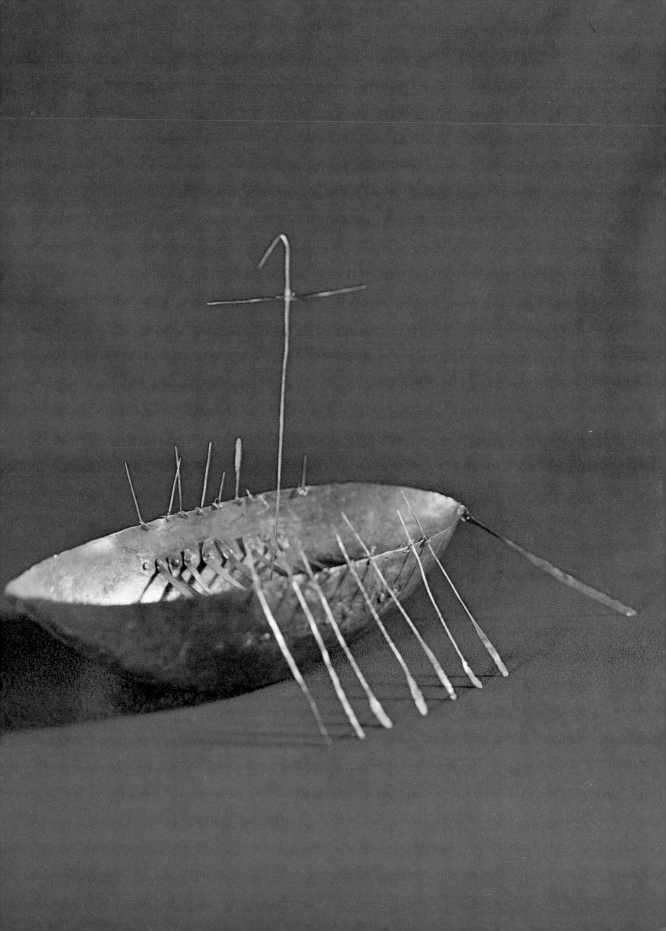

Nestling inside the middle wall at Nendrum are a number of rounded huts. The nearest one housed a bronze workshop.

The massive stone fort, probably Early Iron Age, which dominates the valley at Staigue, Co. Kerry, is the most imposing example of the Celtic fortified circular homestead in Ireland.

show an interesting contrast not only in their size but also in their location at opposite ends of the country.

The monastery of Nendrum is situated on Rahee Island in Strangford Lough in Co. Down. It was originally accessible only by crossing a ford, but it is now linked to the mainland by a bridge. The monastery is thought to have been founded by St Mochaoi in the fifth century and the rest of what we know of its history are the names of some of its abbots, the last known of whom, Setna O Damen, was burned in his own house in 974. Its location was forgotten until the nineteenth century, when Dr Reeves, later Bishop of Down and Connor, was shown the site of an old lime kiln in 1844; by careful probing he was later able to identify it as the Round Tower of the monastic establishment. The two excavations which have been carried out there, the first by H. C. Lawlor in 1922–24, and the second by A. C. Thomas in 1954, have produced more material than any other monastic site in Ireland. The site encompasses three roughly concentric stone walls placed up to thirty metres apart, of which the largest and most ruinous is over five hundred metres long. The excavations were unable to clarify whether these walls were in existence already when the monastery was founded or whether they were built by the monks. Within the smallest of these walls lay the Round Tower, and also the church,

65

of which little more than the foundations remained. It was originally a small church, 7·70 by 5 metres, but was enlarged at the end of the twelfth century. Stone slabs decorated with crosses in relief were found over or near a number of graves which were discovered in the area of the church. Lawlor described one burial as that of a man almost 1·80 metres tall who was lame and 'with right leg and arms well developed, indicating great muscular power; he probably had a loud voice and used it frequently'. How Lawlor was able to deduce the power of the dead man's vocal chords from his skeleton is difficult to say, but he did so in the belief that the man must have been a Viking, and it is interesting that one of the very few Irish inscriptions written in Runic or Viking Scandinavian characters is one found on a stone at Nendrum, which Lawlor possibly thought once covered the grave of the lame man. The inscription reads *Brimabota*, which possibly has something to do with the word 'abbot'. The north side of the area between the innermost and middle *cashel* (surrounding wall) had been levelled at some uncertain date, and round huts with a diameter of about ten metres and a rectangular building were found on this terrace. One of the round huts contained many fragments of crucibles, and was probably the monastic bronze foundry. Inside the rectangular building Lawlor came upon thirty inscribed tablets of slate or stone with designs of varying degrees of competency. One bore the letter 'e', and others had pleasing drawings of animals and birds including one very naturalistic rendering of a seagull. Lawlor concluded that this building must have been the monastic school. With the exception of some pottery which may be sub-Roman, there is little or no material from the site which could be dated with any confidence to a period earlier than the eighth century—three centuries after the alleged date of the founding of the monastery.

It would seem that most of the buildings erected on these early monastic sites were flimsy structures of wood or wattle and daub, which have naturally long since disappeared and which would leave scarcely any trace at all in the ground. The subsequent digging of graves in and around the church ruins caused further destruction of any evidence that might have survived the ravages of time and the elements. But in the rugged areas of the west coast of Ireland, where stone was more easily obtainable than wood, the stone beehive cells and rectangular oratories of the monks have preserved for us a hint of what some of these early monasteries must have looked like. The early monastery dramatically situated near the top

Fragment of a gravestone of the Viking period from Nendrum with the word *Brimabota* inscribed in Runic characters.

In what seems to have been the residential area of the old monastery at Reask, two *clocháns* (beehive huts) are conjoined and overlain by a later straight wall.

of the little rocky island of Skellig Michael off the coast of Kerry is a fine example; another was excavated recently at Reask near the end of the Dingle Peninsula, also in Co. Kerry.

If little is known about the history of Nendrum, nothing is known of Reask. It is one of forty or more small monasteries on the Dingle Peninsula; they are all enclosed by a monastic wall, round or oval, and they sometimes retain their curious beehive huts (*clocháns*), round outside and square inside, sometimes with two 'storeys', and built on the corbelled principle we encountered at Knowth and New-grange 3000 years earlier. Until 1969 the site of the monastery at Reask was owned by three different farmers; but with the aid of the Irish Tourist Board, the Commissioners of Public Works in Ireland were able to take it over and declare it a National Monument, and shortly afterwards they asked a member of their staff, Tom Fanning, to carry out excavations there prior to conservation. The former owners, being old men bound by the ancient traditions and fears, were not interested in working on the site as they considered the place sacred to the fairies. However a number of younger men,

67

Maltese cross and Celtic spiral designs combine to decorate this Early Christian stone pillar-slab at Reask. The letters *dne* inscribed upon it are an abbreviation of *Domine* (Lord).

among them two who had previous experience with the Office of Public Works, were attracted by the money offered plus the prospect of interesting work. With the aid of these men and a number of archaeological students, the excavations got under way.

Each year from 1972 until 1974 you could hear the men talking to each other and to Tom Fanning in their beautiful Kerry Irish, which is a joy to listen to even if you cannot understand it. Before the start of the excavation, the monastery of Reask was celebrated for having provided one of the finest cross-inscribed pillar-slabs in Ireland, dating possibly from the seventh or eighth century. Another five were known to have come from the site, though only one of these still stood there when the excavation began. One of the excavation's successes was the finding of six more of these decorated slabs, which now add considerably to the importance of the site.

A road which has now been diverted to run around the site formerly ran through the middle of the monastery, cutting it into two unequal portions. In 1972–73, Tom Fanning concentrated on uncovering the larger segment. All that was visible above ground were two beehive huts which were in the northern part of the walled enclosure. They had been built together to form a figure of eight, and they were originally interconnected by an internal door, with one external entrance serving both buildings. In the south-western part of the enclosure there were two other conjoined *clocháns*; nearby a souterrain disappeared underground only to emerge again outside the enclosure. There were also traces of iron-working in the form of slag and a number of furnace bottoms.

On this larger portion of the site there were no finds to indicate its religious nature, and had it not been for the inscribed pillar-slabs, the excavator would have been excused if he had doubted whether he was excavating an ancient monastery at all. However, these doubts would have been dispelled in 1973 when Tom Fanning began digging the smaller portion of the site on the other side of the road. Under the surface he found five or six courses of stonework which belonged to a small oratory measuring 3·50 by 2·90 metres. Inside, it must originally have looked like any beehive hut, with the corners rounded off, but it had well-marked angular corners on the outside, giving it the characteristic boat-shape of the oratories on Skellig Michael and at Gallarus. The oratory was built over earlier burials, so that we can conclude that it did not belong to the earliest period of the site, and while it was still in use, other burials were laid out near it. When the oratory was no longer functional, the area surrounding it became a children's burial ground. Unfortunately no material has so far come to light, either in the shape of artefacts or even cross-slabs, which enables us to define exactly when the monastery was built. But the area under the former road still remains to be excavated at the time of writing, and there is always the hope that it may produce something which may provide a clue.

While the monasteries of Early Christian Ireland about which we know something have produced little datable material, the position is reversed to some extent on the secular sites about which we rarely know any history, but which have produced a considerable amount of material, some of which is fairly closely datable. The ring-forts described in the last chapter remained the most common form of settlement throughout this period. But one other type deserves description here not only because of its unusual nature but also because it seems to have been the residence of some of the wealthier lay members of the population. This is the *crannóg*—a structure built of wood forming an artificial island in a lake and which derives its name from the Irish word *crann*, meaning 'tree'.

The very first site excavated by the Harvard Mission to Ireland under Professor Hugh Hencken in 1932 was one of two *crannógs* at a place called Ballinderry on the borders of counties Westmeath and Offaly, and known as Ballinderry I. The existence of the *crannóg* only came to light when, after the accidental discovery of a sword in a ditch during drainage operations, Dr Mahr of the National Museum came from Dublin to inspect the site and discovered further finds including timbers which indicated that here was a hitherto unknown *crannóg*.

When first discovered, the site lay in a somewhat swampy valley, but originally it must have lain in an arm of the nearby lake of the same name. To reach the original ground surface, the excavators had to dig down 4.5 metres below the present water table, and this necessitated damming off the water by blocking up drains and using a water pump. The *crannóg* was an artificial island which was surrounded by a thick palisade 28 by 27 metres in extent, made up of piles which were driven into the ground beneath. Just inside this upright palisade there was a further—and apparently later—palisade of horizontal planks which seems to have partially blocked the main entrance situated on the south-east of the *crannóg*. There was probably another entrance on the north side, outside which lay a quay. Resting on the original lake-bed near the centre of the enclosure there was what looked like a raft made of logs with a girth almost

In excavating Ballinderry I, Hencken carefully numbered each layer of the *crannóg*. Layer 6 shows the level of House I.
Left to right Professor Hencken, Professor Movius and Dr Mahr.

equal to that of telegraph poles. These were laid out in a rough square with each side about seven metres long. It was not a raft they formed, however, but the foundation on which the whole upper structure of the *crannóg* rested. The logs were not attached to one another, and had probably been laid down on dry ground during a season when the water in the lake was comparatively low. This foundation of logs was held in position by some rather large stakes rammed down into the lake-bed below. Above this foundation the builders then piled layers of peat stiffened by timbers and interspersed with brushwood, and on these they built a horseshoe-shaped floor made of timbers, with its entrance facing the main entrance of the *crannóg*. Some of the timbers with which this floor was constructed showed signs of having been cut very carefully into special shapes, but these shapes bore no relationship to the position of the timbers in the *crannóg*; it was obvious that these timbers had been removed from another structure which had been built by carpenters with a high degree of technical skill. But wooden vessels found in the *crannóg* showed that its inhabitants were using utensils which themselves show a detailed knowledge of wood-working. The floor had a diameter of about eighteen metres and over it was spread a layer of brushwood upon which the original inhabitants would have walked and possibly sat. In the middle of the floor was a hearth. We know little about the structure of the house itself, since the house (known as House I) was almost completely demolished after it had subsided to what one can only presume was an unacceptably damp level when the ground of the lake-bed gave under the weight of the timber. However, it is known that one rather large pole rested on the floor of the house and presumably supported a roof of unknown material. When the house was demolished, further layers of peat and brushwood were heaped up where it once stood, and on top of them two further houses—known as Houses II and III—were erected, possibly one after the other. They were however not placed on top of where House I stood, but on either side of it, nestling in the shadow of the palisade of upright stakes at the edge of the *crannóg*.

By correlating tree-rings, the timbers with which the quay outside the northern entrance to the *crannóg* had been constructed were found to have been felled four years later than those of Houses II and III, showing that it was a secondary construction. In the layers of peat and brushwood below the two later houses, Hencken came upon a dug-out boat made from a single tree-trunk and measuring 5.40 metres long, which, because it was below the houses, must have been in use before the quay was erected. It may have been the vessel used by the inhabitants of House I to ferry them across to the artificial island from the mainland when the water level of the lake was normal. When Houses II and III became redundant, the site was covered over by various layers of different materials, which contained finds showing that the site was intermittently occupied until its final abandonment early in the seventeenth century.

But when was the *crannóg* first built and occupied? Another *crannóg* excavated by the Harvard Mission two kilometres away and known as Ballinderry II showed evidence of having been occupied already during the Later Bronze Age, but no such early traces came to light in Ballinderry I. Among the earliest datable finds was a penannular brooch which had been found in the same level as the hearth in House I. It could belong to the seventh or eighth centuries AD. But other discoveries from the same stratum, such as Viking spearheads dating from between 950 and 1050, suggest that it may have been an heirloom when it came to be deposited in the *crannóg*. The sword which had led to the discovery of the site in the first place was also considered by the excavator to have been an heirloom. It was a fine sword with rounded pommel, and with a silver-plated

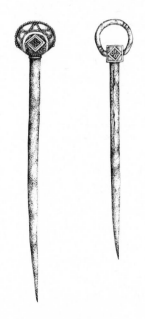

These bronze pins from Ballinderry I were used to fasten clothes in tenth-century Ireland.

The hanging lamp from Ballinderry.

cross-guard decorated with a vine pattern and bearing the name Hiltepreht on its upper surface. The blade of the sword bore another name, Ulfberht. The knuckle-shaped pommel shows the sword to be of a type manufactured around or after 800 AD, and even if it was fairly new when it was brought from the Continent or captured in a fight against the Vikings, it may still have been up to 150 years old when it was lost at Ballinderry.

Besides these items, the two most important finds from the excavation were a bronze hanging lamp and a wooden gaming board. The lamp was found just outside the palisade near the northern corner of House III. It is rounded at one end and pointed at the other, and near the pointed end there is a strainer which partitioned off an area which once contained the lamp's wick. The bowl is decorated with incised marigold patterns and with a plaque bearing plant ornament which helps to date the lamp to around the early ninth century. Possibly more intriguing was the gaming board, which was found in the lowest layer of the peat and brushwood fill which covered House I. The board was made of yew wood and is square in shape. Around the sides there are ornamented panels of interlacing, ring-chain and fret patterns, and single heads of different sizes project from two opposite sides. The central part of the board is perforated with seven rows each of seven holes, thus making a square with a total of forty-nine holes. Of these, the ones at each corner are marked by being enclosed by a quarter circle impressed into the wood. The hole in the centre of the board is also marked by two similarly impressed circles. The excavation did not reveal any gaming pieces which could have been inserted into the holes during the game. It is difficult to know precisely what game was played on the board. Hencken suggested that it was a variant of the game known as fox and geese, in which the fox is in the centre and ten or twelve geese are on the side of the board. The fox can take the geese, but while the geese cannot take the fox, the object of the game is for them to drive the fox into one of the corners so that he cannot escape. More recently, however, Claude Sterckx has suggested that the board was used in the old Irish game called

Manx gaming board
from Ballinderry.

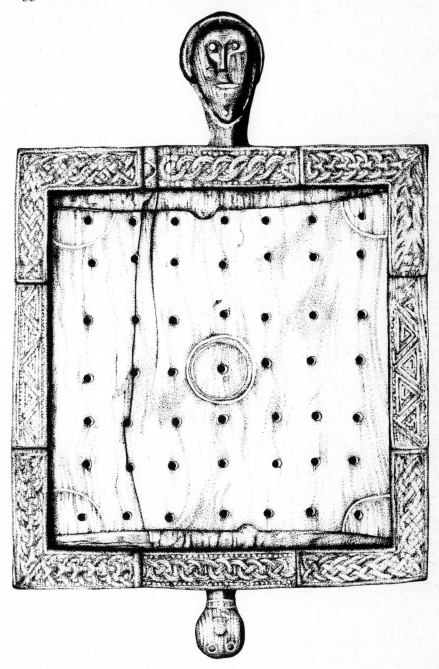

This modern example at Craggaunowen, Co. Clare, completed in 1975, was built to give an idea of the original appearance of a *crannóg*.

brandubh, in which a king stood in the centre of the board surrounded by twelve defenders and attacked from the outside by twenty-four opponents who try to corner him. This game is apparently of Scandinavian origin, and it is interesting, therefore, that the gaming board itself seems to have come from the Isle of Man, where the motifs on the panels surrounding the board are best paralleled and where Viking influence was particularly strong at the time the board was made, around the second half of the tenth century. The route by which the board may have found its way from the Isle of Man to the Irish midlands may have been through the Viking city of Dublin.

The Early Christian period in Ireland, from the fifth to the twelfth century, is one of the richest in the country's record. The products of its many monasteries form one of the focal points of the National Museum's collections in Dublin, and the brilliant techniques of the Ardagh Chalice and the Tara Brooch, as well as the beauty of the many High Crosses on the old monastic sites such as Monasterboice, Co. Louth, bear witness to the very high artistic standard which Irish craftsmen achieved at that time. The Irish church was one of the major forces which kept the spirit of Christianity alive in north-western Europe in the wake of the Barbaric Invasions, and its missionaries helped to spread the gospel in Britain and central Europe in the Dark Ages of the sixth, seventh and eighth centuries. It seems all the more astonishing, therefore, that this great art and this great spirit emanated, not from any one great city, but from a myriad of small and separated monasteries such as Nendrum and Reask. Each of these small monasteries was a cultural centre in itself, often producing its own metalwork, and having its monks studying the Gospels from its own manuscripts, on the margins of which they sometimes wrote nature poetry of remarkable beauty.

The monks led a hard and ascetic life, but the peace and quiet necessary for their spiritual welfare was all too often interrupted by raids carried out not only by the Vikings (whom we shall meet in the next chapter), but also by unfriendly Irish neighbours who were jealous of their possessions. For while the laymen who lived in *crannógs* like Ballinderry were rich dairy farmers, they were also men of war, whose summer occupation it was to gain possession of their enemy's cattle in order to increase their own herds. As such, they therefore needed to defend themselves against their aggrieved foes who, sooner or later, were bound to descend upon them to wreak vengeance and to regain the stolen livestock. They entrenched themselves in *crannógs* which were difficult of access, or behind the ramparts of a strong ring-fort. The thousands of scattered Irish ring-forts and *crannógs* reflect a society of small Irish farmers and petty kings nominally responsible to a High King at Tara who, in fact, rarely had any real power over those whom he regarded as his subjects. It was this fragmentation of Irish society and the desire for independence among each of its members which was the stumbling-block which for long prevented the Irish from presenting a united front in the face of foreign invaders—at first the Vikings, and later the Normans.

6

Viking and Medieval Dublin

Melkorka was an Irish princess, a mere fifteen years old, when she was captured by Viking raiders and sold as a slave (albeit pretending to be a deaf-mute) to an Icelander named Hoskuld. Hoskuld brought her to Iceland with him and there she bore him a handsome son named Olaf the Peacock. One morning when Olaf was two years old, Hoskuld went down to a stream near his house and discovered Melkorka and Olaf talking happily to one another. When he realised that she was not speechless as he and everyone else had thought, he asked her who she was and said that there was no point in concealing her identity any longer. She agreed and said, 'If you want to know my name, I am called Melkorka. My father is called Myrkjartan, and he is a king in Ireland.' When Olaf grew up, he set off to visit his maternal grandfather, and when Myrkjartan (whose Irish name was doubtless Muircheartach) discovered who the visitor from Iceland was, he welcomed him as a member of the family. He brought Olaf with him to Dublin where it caused a great stir that he should be accompanied by the son of the daughter who had been taken captive so long ago.

This charming little story, as told in the Icelandic *Laxdaela Saga*, reflects in some aspects the early history of the city of Dublin, although in fact it would have taken place a century after the city was founded. For while the first encounters of the Vikings with the Irish were undoubtedly hostile raids for the purpose of obtaining booty, the two races intermingled and ended up by living in peaceful co-existence with one another, and this we can see mirrored in the Viking remains which have lately been discovered in Ireland's capital city. These Vikings were bands of rovers and tradesmen who set out from Scandinavia towards the end of the eighth century and descended upon the peoples of northern and western Europe. Aided by the invention of the keel-boat around AD 600, they revolutionised sea-faring, and their fast and seaworthy craft brought them as far as Italy and Constantinople. They settled in England and the Scottish Isles, and carved out kingdoms for themselves in Normandy and Sicily, and discovered America as they voyaged westwards via the Faroes, Iceland and Greenland.

Their first recorded descent upon Ireland took place in 795, and these sporadic raids continued for a full half-century before the Vikings attempted any permanent settlement in the country. The image which they left behind them at the time in the old Irish written records is that of cruel destroyers of monasteries and general disturbers of the peace. But the Irish disturbed the peace just as much and recent scholarship has begun to stress the more positive contributions made by the Vikings to Irish life. Before their arrival, Ireland was a country characterised by isolated settlements of ring-forts, *crannógs* and monasteries. Towns as we know them today did not exist. Yet it was the Vikings who laid the foundations of many of Ireland's coastal towns, starting with Dublin in 841, and continuing with Wexford, Waterford, Cork and Limerick in the following century. These Irish towns, and foremost among them Dublin itself, became important centres of trade, bartering slaves like Melkorka for Arabic silver and other merchandise. Where before there had been occasional fairs for the exchange of goods, the Vikings established permanent markets in Ireland, as is shown by the Norse origin of the Irish word *margadh*, meaning 'market'. In fishing and boating, too, the Vikings contributed words to the Irish language, as they did also in the realm of coinage, for they were the first to mint money in the country, around 997. The Vikings made Dublin into what was probably the most important trading centre in the whole of north-western Europe at the time.

Already in the middle of the last century traces of Viking activity in and around Dublin had been unearthed, the most important of these being graves containing Viking weapons and jewellery which were discovered when foundations were being dug for Kilmainham Hospital and for the railway-line at Islandbridge on the western outskirts of the city. Unfortunately the exact location of these graves was not recorded at the time, but when the Longmeadows War Memorial Park was being laid out at Islandbridge in the 1930s, a further five graves were found, thus giving some indication of

Wattle remains of thirteenth-century houses in the foreground and the leather-workers' quarter on the left in the High Street excavations 1967–71.

where the old cemetery had lain. The graves discovered in the 1930s were not nearly as productive of Viking remains as those found in the previous century had been, but all the finds taken together show the Islandbridge necropolis to have been by far the most important Viking cemetery ever to have been discovered in Britain or Ireland. The inventory of only one complete grave was recorded in the nineteenth century. It consisted of a skeleton, a sword, a spear, an axe, a shield boss and a bronze pin, which represent the typical gear of the early Viking invader. Many of the other unrecorded graves must have been equally rich, for the National Museum of Ireland now houses 40 swords, 26 shield bosses, 35 spearheads and a trader's weighing-scales, all of which came from the graves of these warrior merchants. By a strange coincidence, another Viking sword in the Museum's collection came to light when the foundations for the Museum itself were being dug at the end of the 1880s. But this cemetery was not the last resting place of itinerant marauders. That the people buried there were already permanent settlers is shown by the presence of a number of women's graves, from which the Museum still has buckles, needle-cases and a number of beautiful brooches whose humped oblong form has led to their being called

78

tortoise brooches. A few of these brooches and some of the earliest
swords from the warriors' graves may have been made in the Viking
homelands before there was any permanent Viking settlement in
Dublin at all. This is not to say that the graves date from earlier
than the city's foundation in 841, but rather that these are the graves
of the earliest Viking arrivals in Ireland shortly before the middle
of the ninth century.

At around the same time that the cemetery at Islandbridge and
Kilmainham was being destroyed, T. M. Ray was busy making notes
of other Viking finds which were turning up when he was super-
vising the making of sewers for Dublin Corporation in the area
around Christchurch Cathedral in 1856–59. This was the area which
formed the highest point of the city, and the central part of the
medieval walled town. In one corner of the town lay Dublin Castle,
and just a century after Ray's discoveries, the Office of Public Works
did a small trial excavation under the courtyard of Dublin Castle
and discovered some remains of iron-working, houses of the
eleventh century, and coins of the tenth and eleventh centuries. An
interesting find was a comb fragment with an inscription '*Ane*'
written in the old Irish Ogham script* and dating from around the
eleventh century. The pottery found at this site goes back at least
to the tenth century if not slightly earlier. In 1962, shortly after the
end of these trial diggings, the National Museum started excavations
not two hundred metres away in a triangular area south of Christchurch Cathedral and enclosed by High Street, Nicholas Street and
Back Lane, in advance of Dublin Corporation building a new road-
way there. These excavations were undertaken by Breandán Ó
Ríordáin who continued digging there until 1963. He returned to
the site in 1967 and completed its excavation in 1972. Dublin
Corporation's plans for the area included the building of new civic
offices on a site bordering Winetavern Street and on the slope which
leads northwards from Christchurch Cathedral down to the Liffey
at Wood Quay. The Corporation demolished the old houses which
opened on to Winetavern Street, and while Mr Ó Ríordáin was still
excavating at High Street in 1969, he started digging down under
the foundations of the houses which had just been removed. In the
autumn of 1972, yet a third site became available for excavation.

*Ogham, called after Ogmios, the Celtic god of writing, was the earliest writing in
Ireland, and began probably around AD 300, perhaps as a secret script. The letters are
represented by sets of parallel lines, upright or diagonal, meeting or crossing a straight
baseline.

This was a narrow strip running between Christchurch Place and Ross Road. Whereas normally excavation only takes place during the drier seasons of the year, pressure of development forced the excavation at the Christchurch Place site to continue all the year round under the protection of a polythene shelter, and at the time of writing it is still in progress.

The National Museum's excavations at these three locations in the centre of the old city of Dublin have produced well over 100,000 individual objects—a greater wealth of material than any sanguine archaeologist could ever have imagined even in his wildest pipe-dreams. But it would not have been possible without the patience and co-operation of the city's Corporation; over the years an excellent relationship developed between the excavator and the Corporation officials which has redounded to the great credit not only of the Corporation itself but of the excavator and of Irish archaeology in general, for the excavations have proved to be the most important of the medieval period anywhere in north-western Europe. This is Ireland's first experience of the dangers involved in the modern development of towns inhabited in the medieval period, and one can but hope that the Government will realise the cultural enrichment to the nation of what can be saved by giving archaeologists the wherewithal to meet the challenge where and when it arises in towns throughout the country, and by stipulating that local authorities give sufficient warning of development to allow excavation to take place in good time.

The areas which have so far been excavated by Mr Ó Ríordáin were constantly inhabited over a period of a thousand years, with the houses and refuse of one generation lying on top of that of its predecessors. This piling of layer upon layer meant that air was excluded from the lower deposits and this, combined with the preservative action caused by waterlogging on the site, has meant that many of even the most delicate objects have been almost miraculously preserved where in other conditions they would have long since disintegrated. Unlike the houses of the earlier periods, those of the eighteenth century had cellars which required deep foundations, in the building of which the layers from about 1400 onwards were destroyed. But below these cellars, there remained up to six metres of debris of earlier centuries. Breandán Ó Ríordáin has gone down to the old ground surface in many areas, and one slight disappointment is that so far he has encountered practically no material which can be safely assigned to the ninth century and

Eleventh-century Dubliners walked along this plank pathway, which was about one metre wide.

The intricacies decorating the word *Quoniam* at the beginning of St. Luke's Gospel in the Book of Kells (folio 188r) demonstrate the mastery of Celtic monks in the art of manuscript illumination around 800.

therefore to the earliest Viking settlement. It is possible that the first Viking inhabitants lived in some area around Christchurch Cathedral which has not yet been excavated, or possibly somewhere near the later centre of power at Dublin Castle. It is conceivable, however, that the very earliest settlement lay somewhere further up river from the present site, somewhere nearer where the early graves were discovered at Islandbridge and Kilmainham, so that constant vigilance is needed in the intervening areas for possible traces of the dwellings of those whose graves we know from the nineteenth century.

It must be stressed that despite the extent of the excavations, only a small fraction of the old city within the town walls has so far been uncovered, and because the areas so far excavated are not all situated together, it has not been possible to correlate the sites sufficiently to work out the original street plan. Even on the individual sites it has not always proved possible to trace the streets from one level to another. One thing is certain and that is that the streets were

81

narrower than they are today. They scarcely even merit the name of street, for they were little more than pathways, sometimes paved with stones. More often they were made of wooden boards placed side by side across two split tree-trunks which ran parallel to each other on either side of the path.

The earliest houses were all made of wood. The most popular type was made of two spaced rows of upright posts with horizontal layers of wattles or rods of hazel, ash or elm woven between them in the technique we can see used in basket-making today. They were often plastered with stiff clay to keep the wind and rain out, and while this clay is seldom preserved intact, an excellent example of its use can be seen in one of the houses discovered in Christchurch Place. This house was in use in the late eleventh or early twelfth century, and measured 9.50 metres long and 4.45 metres wide. Its long axis ran east-west, and the doorway was placed off-centre in the south wall, being surrounded by two stout oak jambs on either side. Slots or grooves were normally cut in the side of the jamb opposite the door to receive the wattlework walls of the house. One early house in Winetavern Street was of a different type, and was probably a workshop. It was 4.40 metres long and 1.60 metres wide, and was sunk one metre below ground level. Its walls, consisting of closely-set vertical planks, remained to a height of 30–50 centimetres. The floors of these houses were often covered with wattlework and probably sometimes rushes as well which were gathered from the nearby river bank. The inhabitants presumably cleared each house of what furniture there was before it was demolished, but in one house they forgot to remove a four-legged stool. At first wood was used for making the kitchen vessels such as the wheel-turned bowls, platters and dishes which have been found, and great competence in woodworking and coopering was seen in one example of a lidded vessel built of staves.

In those days there was no organised refuse disposal, and people put their garbage into pits. These pits may not sound very attractive to laymen, but for the archaeologist they provide a mine of information on domestic life at the time, as our own rubbish dumps would provide for the archaeologist a thousand years hence. The animal bones found in the pits show that there was a predominance of pork on the menu, but beef and mutton were introduced occasionally for the sake of variety. Geese, swans, ravens and sea eagles were also caught, and the remains of cockles and mussels provided not only material for meals but for the refrain of one of Dublin's best-

A high standard of carpentry in thirteenth-century Dublin is reflected in this pre-fabricated pit.

known songs. Further details of the daily diet were pieced together by Professor G. F. Mitchell, whose analysis of the seeds in the pits demonstrated that strawberries, apples, cherries, plums, sloes, rowanberries and hazel nuts must have been served up occasionally as the fruit or dessert course. In the thirteenth century this was enriched by the addition of imported grapes and also figs, on which we know taxes were levied. Just how minute and microscopic Professor Mitchell's research was is shown by the fact that among the seeds he also found the remains of a male flea, which so delighted the authorities in the British Museum that they asked for and were granted it on loan to have it put on exhibition! The organic remains found beside the tenth-century body of a girl buried in the boulder clay in High Street, and which presumably came from the girl's stomach, showed that her last meal had comprised a gruel or porridge made from such things as goosefoot and three sorts of *polygonum* which we would today relegate to the realm of weeds.

The finds recovered from the levels dating from before AD 1000 showed many connections with Scandinavia and the Scottish islands. One brooch decorated in the so-called Borre-Jellinge style has almost exact parallels in Sweden and Norway, and small bone pins ending in an animal head are similar to those known already from Scandinavian sites. Furnace slag and baked clay crucibles show the existence of bronze-making workshops at the time, and chippings of amber show that this much-prized material was imported in its raw state from the Baltic and worked on the site in the manufacture of ornaments. The Scandinavian connections of the finds from this period are understandable, because they date from a time in the city's history when the Vikings were using Dublin as a centre for trade with areas outside Ireland, and where their political interests were less with the city's hinterland than with other Viking kingdoms in York, the Scottish islands and in Scandinavia itself.

This picture changed somewhat after Maelschechnaill, the Irish King, roundly defeated the Viking citizens of Dublin in the Battle of Tara in 980, and exacted a large tribute from them. After the Battle of Clontarf thirty-four years later in which the Irish under King Brian Boru defeated the Vikings from Dublin and across the seas, the Viking population of Dublin became less warlike and began to live in much greater peace with their Irish neighbours, while still retaining their Nordic individuality and extensive trade outside Ireland. Thus a handled wooden object resembling a spade or baker's shovel found in Christchurch Place, and coming apparently from an eleventh-century layer, bears a runic inscription *Kirlakar*, which is obviously the Viking name of the owner. Pottery imported at around this period from the Rhineland, from Andennes in Belgium, and from western and north-western France, has recently been identified by the great English medieval pottery specialist, Dr J. G. Hurst. The coins which began to be minted by Sitric Silkenbeard, the Viking king of Dublin, around 997 were possibly used to conduct extensive trade with Anglo-Saxon England, to which a broken strap-tag, a pewter brooch and a tripod pottery pitcher found in the excavations bear witness. The Norman invasion of England may have forced some craftsmen from a Scandinavian settlement in London to emigrate to Ireland, a suggestion which may help to explain how Dublin was able to achieve the high standard of artistic work carried out in the city shortly after this period. Mr Ó Ríordáin has turned up many 'trial pieces' in which carvings ranging from the rudest preliminary sketches to finished patterns were executed on pieces of bone, wood or stone, like those found in the monastery at Nendrum. The best

This gilt-bronze brooch decorated with animal interlace in the tenth-century Borre-Jellinge style was brought to Dublin from Scandinavia.

The thirteenth-century cobblers' quarter contained hundreds of leather soles which had been discarded when shoes were repaired.

of these may have been used for casting the motifs found on contemporary Irish metalwork. Indeed the increased Scandinavian influence felt on Irish metalwork from the middle of the eleventh century onwards may have been due to art work of Scandinavian character having filtered through Dublin or having been made there by Scandinavian and Irish artists working in unison to produce ecclesiastical antiquities for the Gaelic parts of Ireland.

When, immediately after the Norman invasion of Ireland, King Henry II of England held court in Dublin in the winter of 1171–72, he handed the city over to the men of Bristol for colonisation. After this time, the Scandinavian links declined, and much pottery was imported from the west of England, of which the ware made at Ham Green near Bristol is typical. But despite its new rulers, Dublin still continued its extensive trade with western France which it had started at the latest in the eleventh century, and the three Dublin sites have produced more pottery from the Saintonge area near Bordeaux than any other site outside Saintonge itself. One noticeable change in Dublin after the Norman invasion was the concentration of certain specialised craftsmen, possibly already organised in guilds, in certain parts of the city, although this development was already foreshadowed in the earlier periods. Ó Ríordáin's excavations in High Street produced a layer of leather fragments at least 60 cms thick, including the remains of at least a thousand shoe soles. It appears that when the citizens had worn out their soles they brought their shoes to one of the cobblers who removed the soles, but retained the uppers and sewed new soles on to them. Comb-makers were also among the specialised tradesmen whose products have been found in quantities. The antlers of red deer were gathered from where the deer roamed outside the city boundary and were then cut up into plates. These plates then had teeth cut in them and were given a strengthening back or fillet. For richer customers, the comb-makers provided special cases into which the teeth were fitted to keep them intact.

Early Viking decorated weights from Island-bridge.

One rather intriguing find from Winetavern Street was a carefully prepared wood-lined pit which was sunk from the late thirteenth-century layer. It may originally have been used for tanning, but later served as a receptacle for domestic refuse. Its wood provided very interesting material with which to help provide comparative dates for many other wooden structures from the site. In the large timbers it was possible to count the great number of yearly tree-rings, and as the distances between each year's growth of tree-rings varies from year to year, it is possible under ideal conditions to fit the tree-rings of one piece of wood into the pattern of those of another piece of wood. The wood from old Dublin has been examined by Michael Baillie of the Conservation Laboratory in Belfast, and he has been able to correlate many of the timbers in order to build up a complete range of tree-rings over a period of 450 years spanning approximately the years from 850 to 1300. Through this method it is possible to slot any timber into the overall scheme and to work out almost to the year the date of any one building in comparison to any other. So far it has not been possible to date the structures exactly or absolutely, because it has not proved feasible as yet to continue the tree-ring sequence after 1300 and to join it up with that from more recent times. But as soon as Mr Baillie has a set of timbers (not necessarily from Dublin) which will give a complete tree-ring pattern from about 1220 to 1460, he will be able to work out the exact year in which a piece of wood was felled, and will be able to provide a more accurate system for dating the structures and the finds in them than has been possible up to now.

On the basis of this tree-ring chronology, Mr Baillie was able to give a tentative date of around the third quarter of the thirteenth century to the timber of the wood-lined pit from Winetavern Street. In the upper layers of the fill of this structure a coin, an obole of Edward I of Bordeaux (*circa* 1286–1292), was found, and would seem to confirm the approximate dating of the timbers. Immediately below the coin, 2,061 pewter tokens were found together. They bear representations of an ecclesiastic with a crozier, a pilgrim with a staff, an ape with an apple, a pelican and a pair of confronted birds. Dr Michael Dolley, the great coin expert who is Professor of Numismatics at Queen's University in Belfast, has offered an ingenious explanation as to how these tokens came to be deposited in the pit. They were, he says, tokens manufactured in England and imported into Dublin probably to help people pay for small measures of wine which the normal coinage at the time was not sufficiently small to pay for. But shortly after their importation, Edward I introduced the round farthing in 1279, which superseded the tokens and made them illegal. Rather than be caught using illegal tokens, a wine-merchant almost exactly seven hundred years ago must have deposited them in the pit to avoid their discovery, though he must have done so with regret as they contained very nearly a kilo of valuable tin. The find certainly underlines the aptness of the name Winetavern Street.

English pewter tokens which were probably used to pay for drinks in Dublin's Winetavern Street in the thirteenth century.

The preliminary reports of the excavations in old Dublin have already been able to give us a much more intimate picture of the daily life of its citizens during the Viking and Norman periods than any historical documents have ever been able to reveal. The full extent of that picture, fitted together like a jig-saw puzzle from many thousands of pieces, will only emerge whenever the final excavation report is published. But we can already see some of the pieces falling into place. The Islandbridge and Kilmainham cemetery presents us with the remains of the first Viking men and women who came to Ireland from Scandinavia in the second half of the ninth century. The earliest levels unearthed by Breandán Ó Ríordáin around Christchurch Cathedral reveal the trading colony as it was in the tenth century when it was becoming an important centre of international trade. The wealth which commerce and the sword brought to a city like Dublin is reflected more in the gravegoods found at Islandbridge and Kilmainham in the last century than in those parts of the old city which have recently been examined—doubtless because the Vikings of Dublin showed little desire to consign their valuables to rubbish pits or to hide them in the flimsy walls or foundations of their houses. Perhaps these traders' houses do not reflect as fairly upon the quality of Viking carpentry as their ships might if we could but find them intact, and the excavations may not help us to recreate adequately the variety of merchandise which was handled by the Viking traders in Dublin's bustling market place a thousand years ago.

But the few exotic imports and the thousands of locally made pieces recovered in the dig have helped enormously in filling out the background to the town's history. For the first 150 years of its life we see Dublin as a Viking colony which was in closer contact with its distant Scandinavian homeland than it was with its nearest Irish neighbours. But Viking and Irish did not mutually ignore each other. If they often warred against one another, they also occasionally exchanged their wares, and at least by the end of the tenth century, started to intermarry, while the Vikings gradually adopted the religion of their Christian neighbours. By that time, a pattern of integration between the town and its hinterland began to evolve which became more noticeable after the Irish had defeated the Vikings at the Battle of Clontarf in 1014, so that by the end of the eleventh century we seem to find Irish and Viking craftsmen living together in apparent harmony within the town boundary, and cross-fertilising each other with new artistic ideas. The Viking inhabitants taught the Irish something new about trading, coinage and ship-building, and although it took a long time, the Irish did finally learn to appreciate the value of an integrated town, though they never entirely abandoned their age-old settlement pattern of living in isolated homesteads.

With the coming of the Normans to Dublin in 1170, contacts with Scandinavia ceased. Instead, England and in particular Bristol became Dublin's major trading partner, though the Dubliners' appreciation of good claret ensured the continuation of the existing commerce with Bordeaux. In the centuries which followed, Dublin Castle (which was situated at the south-eastern corner of the town) became the centre of Norman power in Ireland, but little archaeological evidence of Norman activity there has so far been revealed. The areas which Breandán Ó Ríordáin has excavated lie outside the castle but inside the town walls. They comprise the hand-workers' quarter, where comb-maker and cobbler were developing their own skills separately and organising themselves into specialist craftsmens' guilds which are the forerunners of the trades unions of today.

The excavation of the old city of Dublin is still continuing, bringing new evidence to light each day, but it is sad to reflect that further work will scarcely help to shed any more light on the period after 1400 as most of the material was swept away in the digging of cellar foundations in the eighteenth century.

This green-glazed jug made in Bristol in the thirteenth century was recently excavated in High Street, Dublin.

7

The Normans
and Cistercians

The Norman occupation of Ireland was by no means confined to the settlement in Dublin. Within thirty years of their arrival, the Normans had conquered large areas of the eastern part of the country with the aid of their superior arms and armour—and a method of conquest not normally practised in Ireland up to that time. The Irish when fighting among themselves were content merely to defeat their enemy and then retire in the knowledge that victory was theirs; in many cases they were happy to make off with the defeated enemy's cattle, without occupying his territory after the battle. The Normans thought differently. What King Henry II had granted to them on parchment they were determined to win by the sword, and unlike the Irish, what they won, they kept. They established themselves on the territory which they took from the defeated Irish by setting up fortifications called mottes; these consisted of a flat-topped mound which looked like an upturned bowl, on top of which they erected a wooden tower called a bretesche. Around one side of the base of the motte they fortified an often crescent-shaped area known as a bailey where the garrison would have left their horses and cattle. Around 1200 they started building stone castles, of which the largest still stands at Trim in Co. Meath. These castles resembled those which the Normans had already built in England and Wales, and their thick walls were more than a match for the swords and spears of the native Irish. The forty or so castles of the thirteenth century which have survived relatively intact in Ireland vary considerably in shape and size, but they all share the display of Norman determination to subjugate the country by means of strong military fortifications. Often, towns grew up

around them and were fortified by a town wall which was attached to the castle.

The Norman conquest of Ireland reached its greatest extent with the invasion of the western province of Connacht in 1235. It was not until the fourteenth century that a combination of native power and comparative lack of Norman financial resources for defensive purposes enabled the Irish to start fighting back effectively against the invaders. By 1400, many of the descendants of the Norman conquerors who had occupied considerable areas of the country had become more Irish than the Irish themselves, and throughout the following century they struggled successfully to gain a considerable amount of autonomy from the English kings. Their territory lay largely in the eastern half of the country where they not only continued to occupy the castles erected by their forebears in the thirteenth century, but also frequently erected new fortifications for themselves which on account of their smaller scale are best described as tower houses. But in the fifteenth century, the native Irish followed suit, and the majority of tower houses which can be seen in their hundreds in the western half of the country were built by native Irish chieftains who wanted to fortify themselves as much against their Irish enemies as against the Anglo-Norman lords in eastern Ireland.

A total of about three thousand castles or tower houses were built in Ireland by Normans or native Irish in the four and a half centuries from 1150 to 1600. Those who built them for the safety of their bodies were equally capable of endowing the building of Cistercian and other monasteries in an attempt to save their souls. The parallel development of castle and monastery in the later Middle Ages in Ireland is exemplified at Trim Castle, Co. Meath and Mellifont Abbey, Co. Louth, where two of the most extensive medieval excavations in Ireland have taken place and where we find a suitable sample of Irish architecture and history in the Norman period.

The massive three-storey tower which we can still see dominating the River Boyne at Trim is a most impressive example of an early Norman fortification, but as the excavations carried out there by David Sweetman for the Office of Public Works since 1971 are already beginning to show, it was not the first Norman fortification on the site.

The Song of Dermot and the Earl, a near contemporary account of the Norman conquest of Ireland, tells us of the erection of the first fortification there by Hugh de Lacy, one of the greatest of the

Between the keep (*right*) and the curtain wall (*left*), David Sweetman's excavations unearthed the rectangular Structure B (*centre*) which straddled a gap in the fosse or ditch surrounding the keep.

Norman conquerors of Ireland, in the following words:

> Then Hugh de Lacy
> Fortified a house at Trim
> And threw a fosse (trench) around it
> And then enclosed it with a herisson (stockade).
> Within the house he then placed
> Brave knights of great worth.

This house was probably a tower built on the site of the existing castle, and the fosse which surrounded it is presumably the deep ditch which David Sweetman has uncovered outside the south-western corner of the existing castle. But the ditch was not continuous, and the level ground between the two ends of the ditch presumably represents the original entrance across the ditch which led to Hugh de Lacy's house within it. Straddling this entrance is an enigmatic building, known as Structure B, which measures 17·50 metres long and about 11 metres wide. It was open at one end, and the lack of finds within this building makes it difficult to guess what its original purpose was. Inside the entrance through the ditch were

93

the foundations of another building, called J, which was destroyed when the present castle was built and thus, like the ditch and Structure B, it would appear to have preceded the building of the present castle. Was this part of de Lacy's original fortification? Again, the lack of finds within the building cannot yet support the suggestion, but it may well have been part of a tower which was demolished in 1212 with the aid of a cable which the historical sources tell us cost twenty-two shillings. This demolition was probably undertaken to make way for the construction of the present Trim Castle; a tall square tower with massive walls 3·5 metres thick, with smaller square towers projecting from the middle of each side of the main tower (only three of these subsidiary towers remain). But while certain features of the castle resemble those used in English castles shortly before 1200, as Roger Stalley has pointed out, the historical evidence suggests that the castle at Trim was not begun until around 1212 when the 'house' mentioned in the song was probably demolished, and when we know that much money was being spent at Trim, presumably for construction purposes. The castle was completed in 1220, probably by Walter de Lacy, Lord of Meath, from whom King John had confiscated the fortifications when he visited Trim in 1210, only to give them back to him five years later—the same year in which the King signed *Magna Carta*.

Walter de Lacy remained the owner of the castle until his death in 1241. He had no male heirs, and the castle passed into the possession of his daughter Matilda, married to an English knight, Geoffrey de Geneville, who made it his demesne manor. It was either de Lacy or de Geneville who built a strong D-shaped curtain wall on the edge of the open space or bailey surrounding the castle. The straight side of this D ran parallel with the river, while the rounded part which defended the castle to the south was further strengthened by having a moat dug outside the wall and filled with water from the river, thus making the castle into an island. In the curved section of the wall there were two gateways and a number of D-shaped towers. When in 1967 the Office of Public Works took over the guardianship of the castle from Lord Dunsany (who still remains the owner), one of these D-shaped towers was bulging dangerously outwards, and it was the need to excavate these towers prior to their repair which brought David Sweetman to work at the castle. The architectural features of these towers suggested a construction date around the middle of the thirteenth century; sure enough, in all three towers that were excavated, thirteenth-century

The foot of the thirteenth-century keep had an inclined plinth added to it some time after it was built. In the foreground is the western end of the ditch which encircled the keep.

pottery came to light, including some fragments of imported French ware and an amount of native pottery. Thirteenth-century blocking walls were also found across the entrances to these towers. Excavations in the western gate-house also produced a considerable quantity of pottery, though much of it would seem to date from the early fourteenth century, and therefore probably some time after the construction of the gate-house. There was a cellar in the gate-house which had no ground-level entrance to it, and the fact that it could only be reached from above suggests that this may have been some kind of dungeon for prisoners.

Before excavation, the ground around the castle sloped away on all sides, and this had led to the suggestion that the sloping ground was the remnant of an original motte thought to have been erected by Hugh de Lacy in 1172. But this ghost was laid to rest as soon as Sweetman put his spade into it. For the sloping ground was not part of a motte, but covered a battered plinth or wall which sloped

95

away at an angle at the bottom of the castle walls. This plinth does not appear to have been erected at the time the castle was built. Underneath it was a layer of earth which extended out from the castle to an area east of Structure B and which contained pottery which had been made at Ham Green near Bristol—the same ware that was also found in the Dublin excavations. The traditional date for Ham Green ware is circa 1240, so that the sloping plinth must have been added to the base of the castle after that date. It is possible that its purpose was to prevent the enemy undermining the walls of the castle. Close to the curtain wall to the south of the castle, and above the layer containing Ham Green pottery, there was a large pile of small chippings which had been thrown away in the cutting of larger stones. It has not been established for which building these larger stones were used. One suggestion is that they were used for the building of the upper part of the castle, the masonry of which seems to differ somewhat from the lower part. But as the top of the pile must once have been beside the curtain wall, it is also possible—if slightly less likely—that the chippings are the refuse from the building of the top of the curtain wall. As the plinth and the chippings date from some time after 1247, Sweetman thinks that it is possible that Geoffrey de Geneville was also responsible for the plinth and whatever part of the fortification complex was constructed with the stones from which the chippings came. However, as he himself is the first to admit, this is mere surmise.

His excavations showed that what is presumed to have been the original ditch of 1172 was filled in, possibly gradually at first, and then completely by some time around the middle of the fourteenth century. Finds from the fill of the ditch included about 20,000 fragments of late thirteenth-century pottery, including French imported ware, a coin of Alexander I of Scotland and a penny of Edward III of England, as well as a French *jetton* of mid-fourteenth century date. A small pit which had destroyed the inner end of the western part of the ditch contained a carpenter's axe and late thirteenth-century pottery.

So far, the excavations have shown few traces of occupation of the castle for almost two centuries following the filling in of the ditch, but these may yet come, as we know that the castle was not entirely unoccupied at this time. Richard II was in the castle in 1399 before he left for England, there to meet his death. He left behind him in ward at the castle two boys aged 8 and 11—Henry of Lancaster, later to become Henry V of Shakespeare's play and

A Ham Green ware jug found at Trim Castle.

the victor at Agincourt, and his cousin Humphrey of Gloucester. Tradition says that they lodged in the gate-house facing the road from Dublin. During the Wars of the Roses (1455–85), the castle was occupied for a time by Richard, Duke of York, who had inherited the castle as a descendant of Matilda de Lacy and Geoffrey de Geneville. He had a tremendous following in Ireland, and many of the Irish barons joined him when he returned to England where he lost his life shortly afterwards at the hands of Queen Margaret, wife of Henry VI, in the Battle of Wakefield in 1461.

The final chapter in the history of the castle was towards the end of the reign of Charles I. In 1647 the castle was strongly refortified by Colonel Fenwicke of the Cromwellian army, and the excavations have shown the extent of his work. The towers which had been excavated in the southern part of the curtain wall had all been filled in during the seventeenth century, and a gun-platform was mounted behind one of them, obviously in preparation for a siege. The material for this infill probably came from various parts of the bailey, and it contained some earlier material such as thirteenth-century arrowheads and even a piece of stained glass. One of the towers produced the gruesome remains of ten skulls which show at the back of the neck clear signs of having been brutally severed from their bodies. Whom the skulls belonged to we cannot say, but they may have been displayed on the battlements *pour décourager les autres* before being flung into the fill of the tower. Structure B, which by this time was many centuries old and probably rather decrepit, was built up again, and the whole of the western half of the bailey was raised to a higher level. But after all these preparations had been made by the Cromwellians for their own defence, the castle fell for a short time into the hands of the Royalist supporters of Charles I in 1649. Despite its great strength, it could only hold out for two days when the Cromwellians besieged it after they had taken the nearby town of Drogheda. After that, it went into a decline and remained in much the same state as it was when David Sweetman started probing to uncover some of the secrets of this great castle which conjures up so much of the history of later medieval Ireland.

Besides castles, the other great buildings of the later Middle Ages in Ireland are the churches, abbeys and friaries. Many of these were built by one or other of the great religious orders which became popular after the middle of the twelfth century, of which the Cistercians were at first the most influential. The Cistercian order

Rowel spur found at Trim. It is unlikely to date from earlier than the fourteenth century.

Above The large galleass in the centre foreground of this cartoon in the National Maritime Museum in Greenwich gives us a vivid picture of what the *Girona* must have looked like when under full sail.
Below The *Girona* proved to be a treasure chest of unique gold ornaments, including (*top centre*) Spinola's gold cross, (*top right*) a gold salamander, and (*centre*) a gold reliquary.

had been founded in Burgundy in 1098, and it introduced a much more austere way of life for monks in order to combat the lax way in which the monastic Rule of St Benedict was being interpreted at that time. The monks got up in the middle of the night to say the Divine Office, and were encouraged to spend part of the day in agricultural pursuits as a counterbalance to the rest of their day which was spent in prayer. One of the order's early disciples, St Bernard, founded his own monastery at Clairvaux (also in Burgundy) and was largely responsible for the rapid spread in the popularity of the Cistercians over wide areas of Europe, including Ireland.

St Bernard's great zeal in his task of reforming the monastic life and the church in general made a great impression on Malachy, the saintly Bishop of Armagh, when he visited Clairvaux in 1139. St Malachy was aware of the fact that the old Irish monasteries of the type we encountered at Nendrum and Reask were as much in need of reform as any other monastery in Europe, and saw in the Cistercians the flame which would rekindle the enthusiasm of the Irish for a stricter observance of the monastic code. So he left behind him at Clairvaux some of his followers to train in the rigorous Cistercian way of life and returned to Ireland in search of a suitable site for a new foundation. He prevailed upon Donnchadh Ua Cerbhaill, king of Airghialla, to grant some land on the Co. Louth bank of the River Mattock where, in 1142, he founded the country's first Cistercian Abbey. He called it Mellifont or, to give it its Latin name, Fons Mellis, the fountain of honey. Malachy then recalled those of his followers whom he had left at Clairvaux to form the Abbey's first community, and St Bernard also sent some of his own French monks to Mellifont to assist them. After a short time, the Irish and French monks fell out, and the latter shortly afterwards returned to France. St Malachy died in the arms of his friend Bernard at Clairvaux on a journey to Rome in 1148, and thus did not live to see the consecration of Mellifont, which took place among a great throng of kings and church dignitaries in 1157. By that time the movement of monastic reform spearheaded by the Cistercians was already well under way, and the old, loosely-organised order of the heroic age of Irish monasticism was no match for it.

At various periods within the last hundred years, excavations had been carried out at Mellifont, but these were on a comparatively small scale and were never adequately recorded. They had at least the advantage of uncovering the main outlines of the church and

Liam de Paor (holding papers) inspecting the excavation of the cloister garth at Mellifont, with the lavabo of *c.* 1200 behind him and the chapter house on the left.

the monastic buildings. As was usual in Cistercian monasteries, these buildings were centred upon a rectangular cloister garth, with the original twelfth-century church on the north side, the chapter house on the east, and the kitchen and refectory presumably on the south side. The north and south transepts of the church were unusual in that they each had three chapels in the east wall—a square chapel in the middle flanked on each side by one terminating in an apse. This arrangement is thought to go back directly to the Burgundian influence of Clairvaux introduced by the French architect Robert, who was one of the monks sent to Mellifont by St Bernard. Perhaps the difficulty in tracing further spheres of Robert's influence in the design of the monastery may be due to the quarrel with the Irish monks and his subsequent return to France.

Although the older excavations recorded that they had got down to old ground level, this was not generally true over the whole area of the monastery. When conservation works were being carried out by the Office of Public Works in 1953, certain trial diggings revealed fragments of medieval floor tiles not in their original position. Rather than have these trial diggings going on unrecorded, the Office of Public Works decided to put the continuous supervision of the site in the hands of Liam de Paor, who at that time was

Architectural Assistant to the Inspector of National Monuments and who is now lecturing in Medieval History at University College, Dublin. This was an important and indeed historic step, for it was the first of the many carefully controlled excavations that have since been carried out at National Monuments by the Office of Public Works. Due to his other commitments at the time, Liam de Paor was unable to give all his time to the excavation, but despite the difficulties, he was able to uncover one of the largest areas of a Cistercian monastery ever tackled in Ireland.

It had been clear before he started that the existing remains showed churches of two different periods, but the reason for the replacement of the first by the second church only became apparent through de Paor's excavation. When he dug down to ground level, he found that the rock on which most of the church was built sloped away steeply at the west end of the church towards the nearby Mattock river. It was there that Mr de Paor found a feature which was unexpected in a Cistercian church. This was a crypt with a floor level about 2·30 metres below the level of the nave. It seems likely that the Cistercians had built the crypt in order to give a solid foundation for the western end of the nave of the church in order to compensate for the lack of a good rock base for it. The crypt must have been rather cramped, but as it had narrow windows which let in a dim light, it must have been used for some purpose. It had an annexe on the north side which may have served as the monastic safe. Before the second church was built at Mellifont, the crypt was filled in. At the very bottom of this fill there was a considerable amount of charcoal which must have come from the burning wood of the ceiling of the crypt. As another and even more extensive layer of charcoal was found in the east range of the cloister, it was obvious that considerable parts of the abbey had been burned and probably destroyed by an extensive fire, and this was apparently the reason why it was necessary to rebuild the church on the same spot.

But when did this rebuilding take place? A hoard of fifteen coins was found in somewhat charred condition at the bottom of the fill of the crypt in the charcoal layer which rested immediately upon the floor. The coins had been minted in the late twelfth and early thirteenth centuries, and belonged to types which had been demonetised, that is, divested of their value, in Ireland not later than 1251. The coins did not lie together but were scattered over an area almost one metre square. The ingenious explanation for this, suggested by

An aerial view of Mellifont demonstrates the plan of a typical Cistercian monastery, with a church at the northern end of the cloister garth, the chapter house on the east, and refectory and kitchen to the south.

the excavator and by the coin expert Michael Dolley, was that the coins had been hidden in a chink in the rafters forming the ceiling of the crypt, and had lain there until the rafters caught fire in the conflagration which not only scorched the coins but scattered them over the floor when the blazing beams collapsed. Thus it would be wrong to jump to the conclusion that these coins can date the time of the burning of the first church and the building of the second. The coins very probably remained hidden for decades until the fire dislodged them. But the rest of the fill contained pottery which dated from the late thirteenth and possibly early fourteenth century, which suggested that the second church was scarcely built before 1300, and probably a little after that date. It would be tempting to link the burning of the abbey with the name of Edward Bruce of Scotland who was on the rampage in the area around 1315 in his efforts to obtain a solid foothold in Ireland from which to fight the English. But we know also that the de Verdons—neighbouring

Norman landlords—ravaged and plundered the lands of Mellifont three years earlier, and they could equally have been responsible for the destruction. We now have no means of identifying the perpetrators of the deed, but it does seem likely that one or other of these may have been responsible for the destruction of the first church. Thus the building of the second church probably took place some time shortly after 1315, a date which could be supported by the architectural details of the second church. The chapter house extension, which still stands, probably dates from this period too.

The only other building still standing to any height at Mellifont today is the beautiful lavabo, or monks' washing place, on the south side of the cloister garth opposite the entrance to the refectory. It was built around or shortly after 1200, and it is interesting that Liam de Paor found fragments of a lead pipe which ran under the nave of the church and out into the cloister and which was presumably designed to bring water from the river into the fountain of the lavabo. The massive pillars of the crossing—that part of the church where nave and transepts meet—were strengthened in the fifteenth century, probably in order to bear the extra weight of a square tower added at that time. Nothing remains of the tower today. In fact, other than the foundations, very little remains of either of the two churches built at Mellifont, both of which must have been splendid structures in their day.

St Malachy's intuition in having introduced the Cistercians to Ireland at Mellifont proved very astute, for it brought a great new

A silver paten and a chalice of mid-thirteenth century date, possibly made in England, were found with a disturbed burial in the eastern end of the church at Mellifont.

impetus to Irish monastic life which was to last for four centuries until the Reformation. In the century and a half which followed the foundation of Mellifont, thirty-seven other Cistercian houses were created in Ireland. Within a short time, the reforming spirit of the Cistercians was assisted by the arrival of new orders such as the Augustinians, Dominicans, Benedictines and Franciscans. The ordered and organised life of these foundations, and the regular architectural plans of their monasteries laid out around the cloister garth, stood in stark contrast to the individualistic nature and haphazard layout of the earlier Irish monasteries, and the Irish were so attracted to this reformed monasticism that they flocked to the hundreds of abbeys and friaries of the new orders which sprang up all over Ireland in the centuries after the foundation of Mellifont. This great train of renewal was kept in motion until Henry VIII suppressed the monasteries in the years after 1536, in his efforts to get his hands on their lands and possessions which by that time had become quite extensive. The struggle of the Irish monks and laity to retain their religion during the ensuing period of the Reformation was associated with a political battle for Irish independence in which the Irish hoped, but hoped in vain, for successful aid from foreign powers such as France and Spain.

8

'I have Nothing More to Give Thee': the Spanish Armada

A tragic accident of history has given Ireland an extra chapter of archaeology—the salvage of the remnants of what was once the largest and most formidable fleet the world had ever seen: the Spanish Armada. When this *Felicissima Armada* (Most Fortunate Fleet) sailed down the Tagus from Lisbon at the end of May, 1588, it consisted of 130 ships, carrying 28,000 men—over 1,300 generals, captains and officers, 24,000 seamen and soldiers, over 800 ecclesiastics and an untold number of galley slaves. The elite of Spain's nobility was on board, intent on glory and revenge against Protestant England. Half of the ships were galleons—merchant ships adapted for use in war, like the *Trinidad Valencera*; there were 25 unwieldy hulks to carry stores and provisions, and in addition there were four galleys and four galleasses (a cross between sail-driven galleons and oar-propelled galleys) like the *Girona*.

By the time the great fleet had run the gauntlet of adverse weather and the harassing tactics of the smaller but more manoeuvrable English navy up the Channel, it was in serious disarray. The commander, the Duke of Medina Sidonia, who had hardly ever been to sea before, ordered the fleet home. It meant sailing northwards first to round Scotland; and because of unexpectedly fierce autumn gales, only about half of the great fleet ever found its way back to Spanish waters. At least twenty ships, perhaps as many as twenty-six, foundered on the inhospitable coasts of Ireland. Strong westerly winds had forced them on to a lea shore, and scurvy, lack of fresh water and rotting food had drained the crews of so much of their strength that they were almost helpless to save themselves. Even those who managed to struggle ashore were often treated

The *Santa Maria de la Rosa* sank in the sound between the end of the Dingle Peninsula and the Blasket Islands in the right background.

execrably by the Irish inhabitants, who massacred the survivors for any jewels and valuables they might have; and the same fate befell those who were caught by Queen Elizabeth's troops, though not before the English had squeezed every ounce of information they could out of them.

The story of the many attempts, both successful and unsuccessful, to locate and salvage the Spanish wrecks on the coasts of Ireland is a chequered one. In southern Ireland at present, the question of the ownership of wrecks is still covered by the antiquated British Merchant Shipping Act of 1894, though new legislation is promised. Under this old law, any items which are salvaged are to be notified to the local Receiver of Wreck, whose job it is to ascertain the legal owners, if any. Once this has been established, the salvor may, if he can, come to an agreement with the owners and get a fee for salvaging the wreck. But while the Spanish Government would appear to be the rightful claimants to Armada wrecks, the question of their ownership has never been legally settled, and some disgraceful incidents have taken place between rival groups of divers intent more on finding treasure than furthering the cause of archaeology underwater.

In 1963, Desmond Branigan, the doyen of Irish underwater archaeology, began to search for sunken ships in the Blasket Sound, off the extreme south-western point of Ireland. He was acting as researcher for Sydney Wignall, who had already made a name for himself as the leader of the Welsh Himalayan expedition of 1955, and had also worked on several underwater archaeological expeditions in the calmer waters of the Mediterranean. Branigan had done a great deal of research into the documentation of the lost Armada ships, and now he was looking for traces of the *Santa Maria de la Rosa*, the vice-flagship of the Guipuzcoa squadron, which had left Lisbon armed with twenty-six guns and with well-nigh three hundred men aboard. According to contemporary reports, the *Santa Maria* had limped into the Blasket Sound on September 21 1588 with her sails in ribbons. She struck a submerged rock and sank almost immediately. The only survivor was the pilot's son, Giovanni di Manona from Genoa, who drifted ashore on some wreckage and was captured by the English. Before he was executed, he told his captors that the ship had carried at least 15,000 ducats in gold and the same in silver, and 'much rich apparel and plate and cuppes of silver'.

This was all that Desmond Branigan had to go on—this, and the

A diver at work on the *Santa Maria*, carefully recording the remains of the wreck on a calibrated metal grid.

fact that about 150 years ago, some Blasket Islanders had fished up a cannon (now lost) bearing a coat of arms. But it was to be 1967 before what were alleged to be two pieces of iron ballast were found by a rival group searching for the same wreck; and it was not until 1968 that Wignall, armed with a seven-year licence from the Spanish Government which gave him exclusive salvage rights, began a full-scale search for the *Santa Maria de la Rosa* in the Blasket Sound.

After surveying almost fifteen million square metres of the Sound by means of a new 'Swim Line' system devised by Lieutenant Commander John Grattan, a Royal Navy diving expert, Wignall's team of divers came upon two piles of what looked like stones but which, when scratched with a knife, revealed themselves to be concretions that had formed around cannon balls. On top of them lay seven boat-shaped ingots of lead engraved with Spanish characters—ingots of the kind used on board ship to make small-arms ammunition. There were also what seemed to be the remains of five anchors, some animal bones (probably horses and dogs), and a great number of pieces of iron and lead shot for weapons such as culverins, demi-culverins and arquebuses. The remains of one cannon-ball, eleven cms in diameter, may have been an English shot, as it was found lodged among the timbers of the hull of the *Santa Maria* which is known to have been shot at by the English.

Next season, in 1969, after fighting off rival divers in the courts, Wignall was able to resume work on the wreck. Under the piles of concreted ballast, a considerable portion of the lower forward section of the hull was found intact. The keelson (the ship's inner keel) was well preserved, as was the stepping-box of the mainmast. The stern part of the ship seemed to have disappeared; but the evidence suggested that the ship had struck a rock amidships just aft of the mainmast, and the stern had pivoted on impact, broken away, and separated at an angle. The excavators concluded from the existing remains that the ship must have been about twenty-seven metres long, with her mainmast well forward, as was common with ships designed for Mediterranean sailing conditions. Convincing proof that the wreck was, in fact, that of the *Santa Maria de la Rosa* came with the discovery of two pewter plates with the name 'Matute' inscribed on the rim. The sole survivor of the disaster, Giovanni di Manona, had told the English that 'Matuta was the Captain of the Infanterie of that ship.'

No cannon were found on the *Santa Maria*, although the fragmentary remains of six matchlock arquebuses were recorded. Other finds included a silver coin and a double *escudo* of Philip II of Spain, and from the area where the ship's galley would presumably have been located came the brass pan of a pair of weighing-scales, a number of sheep, cattle and chicken bones, and, for the gourmets on board, a Brazil nut in a surprisingly good state of preservation.

In 1970, the first of several (so far unsuccessful) attempts was made by members of the Irish Sub-Aqua Club to locate the wreck of the *Falcon Blanco Mediano*, which sank on September 22 1588 off the island of Inishbofin in Co. Galway. It was a vessel of three hundred tons, had a crew of a hundred and three, and was armed with sixteen guns. What was believed to be one of her guns was dredged up near the presumed site of the wreck in 1740, and was later brought to Westport House in Co. Mayo, where it still remains. Although the cannon is almost certainly not from the Armada, but from an English ship of the seventeenth or eighteenth century, the Inishbofin site will doubtless continue to attract further attention

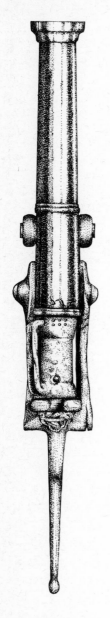

A well preserved loading swivel gun from the wreck of the *Trinidad Valencera*.

Members of the City of Derry Sub-Aqua Club lower one of the bronze 50-pound cannon from the *Trinidad Valencera* into a pit for washing and conservation treatment.

in the years to come until the *Falcon* is located and salvaged.

1971 saw another dramatic success, however, with the finding of the *Trinidad Valencera*. The *Trinidad*, a large Venetian merchantman of 1,100 tons which had belonged to the Grand Duke of Tuscany before she was commandeered and converted for the Armada in Lisbon harbour, had staggered into Kinnagoe Bay at the mouth of the Foyle Estuary in Co. Donegal nine days before the *Santa Maria de la Rosa* sank in the Blasket Sound. She was leaking badly and seemed beyond repair. In calm water, she grounded on a reef sixty metres from shore. Within forty-eight hours the men had disembarked themselves and any treasure they had brought; shortly afterwards she sank—the only Armada ship that is known to have sunk at anchor. What they had not removed was the ship's arsenal; with a total of 42 guns, she had been one of the most heavily armed vessels in the fleet. In February 1971, members of the City of Derry Sub-Aqua Club who had been searching Kinnagoe Bay for two years suddenly saw a cannon muzzle pointing at them from the rocks on the seabed.

The importance of the *Trinidad Valencera* to underwater arch-aeology lies in the recovery so far of four of the finest and best preserved cannon known from the Armada. Two of them were a magnificent matched pair of fifty-pounders, which bore the arms of Philip II of Spain and Mary Tudor of England, the words *Philippvs Rex*, and the date 1556. They had been cast at Malines, the King's gun foundry in the Spanish Netherlands, by the bronze founder Remigy de Halut, whose name is also inscribed on the weapons. Two others were of the culverin family, slender, long-range pieces, and one bore the letters 'ZA'—probably the initials of Zuanne Alberghetti, a gun founder of the great arsenal of Venice. These were presumably part of its original armoury, while the two Spanish whole cannon from Malines must have been mounted when the *Trinidad* was being fitted out for the Armada in Lisbon. They had been carried on gun carriages on deck, the six spoked wheels of which have been identified amongst the wreckage on the seabed.

But the most successful and spectacular achievement of Irish underwater archaeology so far has been the location and salvage of the galleass *Girona*. It reads like a detective story, with all the drama and tragic glamour of an epic historical novel; and indeed, it was a detective story—one, moreover, that has set new standards for underwater archaeology in Britain and Ireland.

Full credit for the location and exemplary excavation of the *Girona* goes to one man—a young Belgian diver and amateur historian called Robert Sténuit. He had become a professional diver in 1964, and for a time he held the world record for depth diving; but all the time he dreamed of the moment when he could mount an underwater archaeological expedition of his own, and to that end he pored over books and documents looking for references to ships with valuable cargoes which had sunk not far from shore. In the card-index of wrecks which he compiled over the years, the *Girona* was marked with three stars . . .

The story of the *Girona* is the tragedy of the Armada in micro-cosm. It centres on a young nobleman called Don Alonso Martinez de Leiva, commander of the *Santa Maria Encoronada*. He had sailed with half the youthful nobility of Spain on board, destined to lead the chivalry of Spain to glorious victory on English soil. He had also been picked to take over the command of the Armada in the event of the Duke of Medina Sidonia's death. Naturally, the English were particularly interested in learning the whereabouts of

Two Spanish coins from the wreck of the *Girona*.

From the *Girona*:
Renaissance lapis
lazuli cameo of a
Byzantine emperor
framed by gold and
pearls.

such an important prize, and it is from their intelligence reports that we can trace the events that led to his death.

The *Santa Maria Encoronada*, much battered by the weather, reached Ireland early in October 1588, whereupon de Leiva anchored in Blacksod Bay off the Mayo coast to take aboard fresh water. His ship ran aground there, but de Leiva was able to bring his four hundred men ashore before setting fire to her. From Blacksod Bay he marched north to Elly Bay, inside Belmullet, where another Spanish ship, the *Duquesa Santa Ana*, had taken refuge. The *Duquesa* was an unwieldy transport ship with 350 men aboard; but de Leiva was able to squeeze his four hundred men plus their valuables on board as well.

Soon afterwards, the *Duquesa* left her safe anchorage south of Belmullet to brave the Atlantic swell once more. She was forced to sail northwards in a storm until she was finally driven ashore on to the beach at Loughros More Bay, near Rossbeg, in Co. Donegal. Once again de Leiva survived, and was able to lead ashore the whole ship's complement—now swollen to nearly eight hundred men—bringing with them whatever valuables and victuals could be salvaged. The Spaniards were now in the friendly country of the Irish 'rebel', MacSweeney na Doe, and for a week they were able to camp there unmolested while his couriers went in search of other Spanish ships. Soon news came that the *Girona* was lying at anchor not very far to the south, at Killybegs.

De Leiva himself had sustained a serious leg injury by this time. But undaunted, he had himself carried in a sedan chair over the hills to a triumphant reunion at Killybegs, where he set about organising the repair of the damaged *Girona*. The *Girona* was a galleass of the Neapolitan squadron which had left Lisbon well victualled and well armed, carrying five hundred men and fifty pieces of bronze ordnance to defend herself, but the autumn storms had taken their toll of her sail and rigging. De Leiva knew that not even the *Girona* could carry 1300 men safely to Spain in the face of the approaching winter storms. His one hope of salvation lay in making for Scotland, where King James VI (son of Mary Queen of Scots) was thought to harbour Catholic sympathies still. So with this presumably in mind, he sailed northwards around the Bloody Foreland on October 26, and headed east for Scotland. But in the darkness of the following night, the *Girona* strayed too close to the shore, struck a reef, and sank within minutes. A third shipwreck was too much even for de Leiva's luck: he and nearly every single one of his 1300 men went down with the *Girona*, and a handful of survivors told the tale to the English.

But where exactly had the *Girona* gone down? According to a report which reached the Queen's Deputy in Dublin three weeks later, the vessel had foundered on the rock of Bunboys on the Antrim coast, and this report has sent many a modern treasure-seeker diving for the wreck at Bunboys, which is near the mouth of the Bush River. But that report seems to have been designed to mislead the English and prevent their salvaging the *Girona*'s guns, and when Robert Sténuit came to research the problem, he preferred to believe the evidence of local traditions enshrined in suggestive place-names marked on the Admiralty charts near the Giant's Causeway, some way from the mouth of the Bush River—names like Port na Spaniagh (Spaniard's Port) and Spaniard's Cove, between which lay a protruding rock known locally as Lacada Point.

In June 1967 Robert Sténuit set off in a small inflatable dinghy with a Belgian friend, Marc Jasinski, a photographer who had already developed special cameras for underwater work. His hunch paid off at once: diving at Lacada Point, on the very first day he found a lead ingot with five crosses on it. Soon afterwards he found a copper coin and two bronze cannon, a portion of a gold chain and three silver coins, one of which bore the letters 'TO', standing for the Toledo mint. There could be little doubt about it: Sténuit had located the wreck of the *Girona* at his first attempt.

Over the next two seasons, Sténuit had to go through the usual court processes—and the usual skirmishes with rival diving groups—before he could establish his rights as sole salvor of the wreck he had located. Everything he found was meticulously recorded, and a list dutifully sent off every week to the local Receiver of Wreck in Coleraine. Legally, if the rightful owner did not claim the treasure within a year, it could be sold by the Crown and the salvor could then claim a fee for having rescued it. During those two diving seasons of 1968 and 1969, Sténuit and his small team not only brought up a veritable treasure chest of finds; they charted and photographed the position of every storm-tossed item on the seabed and were thus enabled to produce a model excavation report on the archaeology of the wreck.

In all, Sténuit recovered a staggering total of 405 gold coins, 756 silver and 115 copper coins, from eight different countries, some of them hailing from Naples, the home port of the *Girona*. But apart from the coins, and the painstaking charting of the positions of the

Robert Sténuit (*left*) shows a silver candle-stick, coins and other finds from the *Girona* to some of his diving team.

finds that allowed Sténuit to make firm conclusions about the way in which the ship had struck and foundered, it was the personal valuables of the flower of Spain's nobility that strike the most responsive chord in the layman's mind. There were two navigating instruments known as astrolabes, of which only twenty-six other examples are known in the world. There were broken knives and forks, fragments of dishes and goblets, candlesticks and a fine set of cameos depicting Byzantine emperors. There was a gold salamander (probably a charm against fire) which seemed to wink an eye at Sténuit every time he looked at it. There was a gold-plated dolphin, and a number of decorated sword pommels.

There was a ring bearing the inscription '*Madame de Champagney* MDXXIIII' (1524). After enormous research, Sténuit discovered that she had been the daughter of the Lord of the Manor of Champagney in Burgundy whose beauty was a byword as far north as the Spanish Netherlands; she had married Nicholas Perrenot, the Minister and Chancellor of Charles V, and one of her sons became Cardinal Granvelle. One of the participants in the Armada, it turned out, was a nephew of this Cardinal . . .

OPPOSITE
Robert Sténuit proudly
holds one of the astro-
labes of the *Girona*,
which he had just dis-
covered on the seabed.

There was a Maltese gold cross with a pointed object between each of the arms. Sténuit discovered that one of the people aboard the *Girona* was a captain named Fabricio Spinola from Genoa: *spinola* in Spanish means 'thorn', and the thorn on his family coat of arms had exactly the same shape as the pointed object on the Maltese cross.

But the most poignant object that Sténuit found was a small ring that highlights all the great personal tragedy which the disastrous Armada expedition must have brought to the thousands who waited in vain for the return of their loved ones. The ring had been worn by a young Spanish nobleman, newly betrothed; for inside it were inscribed the simple words—*No tengo más que dar te*—'I have nothing more to give thee.'

Sténuit wanted the whole collection of finds to stay together. After negotiations with the Crown and the Ulster Museum in Belfast, it was decided that the nation should buy it, rather than have it auctioned separately. Helped by a very considerable grant from the British Government, the Ulster Museum raised the necessary money through public subscription. Robert Sténuit was paid the sum of £132,000 for his labours—very much less than he could have got at a public auction—and in July 1972 the *Girona* treasures went on permanent display in the Ulster Museum in Belfast. Underwater archaeology in Ireland had come of age.

EPILOGUE

Archaeological material of the period after AD 1600 has on occasions been excavated by Irish archaeologists. But this was more by chance than by design, as it happened to lie on top of earlier finds which were usually the object of the excavator's attention. While the Irish Society for Industrial Archaeology has, within the last decade, been gathering together an increasingly wide circle of devotees interested in the archaeology of the nineteenth century, what is described as 'post-medieval archaeology' can be said to have only just begun in Ireland.

But if there has therefore been very little activity in the archaeology of Ireland's recent past, it can truly be said that the future of Irish archaeology is rosy. When we consider that there is little likelihood of the discovery of any great amount of historical documents which will help shed new light on Ireland's ancient history, we realise that archaeology remains the only likely source of providing a large and undiscovered body of evidence which will materially increase our knowledge of the country's past. In recent years, the natural sciences have aided considerably towards the accumulation of accurate data in reconstructing the life and times of bygone eras, as instanced by the development of radiocarbon dating and the correlation of tree-rings in different pieces of timber. Even the study of such apparently insignificant items as snails can supply valuable evidence in determining things like the climate prevalent at any particular period. By using these aids prudently, and with the assistance of substantial state grants towards excavations (though unhappily not so much towards pure research), Irish archaeologists have been rapidly building up an increasingly accurate picture of their country's past, and there is little reason to doubt that they will continue to do so with even greater effectiveness in the future.

BOOKS FOR FURTHER READING

EVANS, E. E., Prehistoric and Early Christian Ireland. A Guide (Batsford, London 1966)

HARBISON, P., Guide to the National Monuments in the Republic of Ireland (Gill and Macmillan, Dublin 1975)

HENRY, F., Irish Art, 3 vols (Methuen, London 1965–70)

HERITY, M., Irish Passage Graves (Irish University Press, Dublin 1974)

LAING, L., The Archaeology of Late Celtic Britain and Ireland *c*. 400–1200 AD (Methuen, London 1975)

LEASK, H. G., Irish Castles and Castellated Houses (Dundalgan Press (W. Tempest), Dundalk 1964)

LEASK, H. G., Irish Churches and Monastic Buildings, 3 vols (Dundalgan Press (W. Tempest), Dundalk 1956–60)

LUCAS, A. T., Treasures of Ireland. Irish Pagan and Early Christian Art (Gill and Macmillan, Dublin 1973)

MARTIN, C., Full Fathom Five (Chatto and Windus, London 1975)

MOVIUS, H. J., The Irish Stone Age (Cambridge University Press, London 1942)

NORMAN, E. R. and ST JOSEPH, J. K., The Early Development of Irish Society. The Evidence of Aerial Photography (Cambridge University Press, London 1969)

Ó RÍORDÁIN, S. P., Antiquities of the Irish Countryside (Methuen, London, 1953)

PAOR, M. and L. DE, Early Christian Ireland (Thames and Hudson, London 1958)

RAFTERY, J., Prehistoric Ireland (Batsford, London 1951)

RAFTERY, J. (*ed.*), The Celts (The Mercier Press, Cork 1964)

STÉNUIT, R., Treasures of the Armada (David and Charles, Newton Abbot 1972)

Viking and Medieval Dublin. Catalogue of Exhibition (National Museum of Ireland, Dublin 1973)

INDEX

INDEX